on track ...
Rush
1984-2015

every album, every song

Richard James

SONICBOND

sonicbondpublishing.com

Sonicbond Publishing Limited
www.sonicbondpublishing.co.uk
Email: info@sonicbondpublishing.co.uk

First Published in the United Kingdom 2025
First Published in the United States 2025

British Library Cataloguing in Publication Data:
A Catalogue record for this book is available from the British Library

ISBN 978-1-78952-372-0

Typeset in ITC Garamond Std & ITC Avant Garde Gothic
Printed and bound in England

Graphic design and typesetting: Full Moon Media

Follow us on social media:
Twitter: https://twitter.com/SonicbondP
Instagram: www.instagram.com/sonicbondpublishing_/
Facebook: www.facebook.com/SonicbondPublishing/

Linktree QR code:

on track ...

Rush

1984-2015

every album, every song

Richard James

SONICBOND

sonicbondpublishing.com

on track ...

Rush

1984-2015

Contents

The Story So Far ...

In under a decade of recording and touring, Rush established themselves as one of the world's hardest-working and most interesting rock bands. By 1983, two significant changes to their previous modus operandi were in place: firstly, 1982's *Signals* had set the band in a new direction. An increased use of, and apparent reliance on, keyboards, together with a compositional bias away from their previous prog rock style towards a more pop, ska and reggae-based sound, had alienated some of their fan base.

The second major alteration was the disappearance of long-term producer and unofficial fourth member of the band, Terry Brown. Brown's contribution to the music of Rush should never be underestimated. From his sonic saving of the debut album, via the fashioning of strange, wonderful, new sound worlds throughout the 1970s, to the major breakthrough of 1981's *Moving Pictures*, his skills behind the desk were instrumental to the band's unique sound. In the band's ascent up rock's ladder (no relation), Brown had been integral to the band's success thus far.

It was not only some reviewers and fans who were unhappy with *Signals*; the band had been unimpressed with Brown's production. For his part, Brown was not keen on Rush's drift away from their highly individual 'hard rock with chops' sound. With Lee and Peart (and, to a lesser extent, Lifeson) wanting to keep in step with the synth-oriented approach, it was inevitable that there would be a parting of the ways. The growing interest in the ever-increasing abilities of keyboard technology and the band's absorption of the musical trends of the day meant that Brown would not return to the producer's chair for any of the albums discussed in this book. This factor alone meant that the band's sound changed dramatically, as did the style, and on occasion, the quality of their songwriting. In *Contents Under Pressure*, Alex admitted:

> Certainly on *Signals*, there was a conflict, I think, between the guitar and the keyboards we were using. For me, that's always been a bit of a sore spot, that record. Because I think there's good material on there, but I think the production on it is lacking. To me, that record doesn't sound that great, from a guitar point of view. We were just really starting to get into keyboards, and I don't think we were well-balanced on that record. And I think that's part of the reason we had decided to move on, in terms of what producer we were going to work with. We wanted to get a little more influence from other people.

In *Chemistry*, Terry Brown recalled:

> It was all becoming very electronic. I had arrived at the point where I couldn't contribute more; if that was the direction they were going in, it just wasn't my forte. The keyboard thing was becoming overtly the band sound,

which I didn't think was cool either. There wasn't a big incident, but I think the writing was on the wall. There were some edgy moments, which were very unusual for us.

At the time, puzzled by the new direction, I became gradually less interested in the trio's output, despite still buying everything they released. However, this was a new Rush, different in both look and sound, progressing musically, and reflecting the times in which they were living.

Grace Under Pressure (1984)

Personnel:
Alex Lifeson: guitars, synthesisers
Geddy Lee: vocals, bass and synthesisers
Neil Peart: drums, percussion and electronic percussion
Recorded at Le Studio, Morin Heights, Quebec, Canada, between November 1983 and March 1984
Produced by Rush and Peter Henderson
Released: 12 April 1984
Label: Mercury Records
Chart positions: Canada: 4, US: 10, UK: 5
All music composed by Lee and Lifeson, with lyrics by Peart

To promote *Signals*, Rush toured from September to December 1982, then took two months off for rest and reconsideration. By the end of the tour, an inter-band agreement had been reached. The synths would still be a part of the sonic arsenal, but to a lesser extent. The guitars would have a fairer share of the mix, and any new producer would be expected to deliver this. 1983 was to be a significant year.

The band picked Steve Lillywhite, who had worked with U2, XTC, Psychedelic Furs and Big Country (although not simultaneously). Writing sessions had taken place at the Horseshoe Valley rehearsal studios in Southern Ontario. Just before the band decamped again for Morin Heights, Lillywhite withdrew from the project, for reasons which have never become clear. In a 'Mohr Stories' podcast interview available on YouTube, Lillywhite said:

> Oh God, Rush hate me ... Because I'd said I'd produce them, then I didn't. The only time I've ever almost been threatened with having my legs broken in the music business ... by their manager!'

Perhaps don't let down one of the biggest rock bands in the world when you agree to become their producer. Just a thought, Steve.

Pressure was mounting with a deadline date for the album's release. Many possible replacements were interviewed, with the task finally going to Peter Henderson, who had recorded Supertramp, Jeff Beck and Frank Zappa. In *Contents Under Pressure* by Martin Popoff, Geddy described the experiences of searching for a new producer and of working with Henderson:

> (Peter) had a vast amount of engineering and co-producing experience with Supertramp and various artists. And his taste in music was right up our alley, and he seemed like a good guy. We went into the studio to start making the record, and we realised he couldn't make a decision. So, it was very frustrating because we had to make all the decisions all of a sudden. And it turned out we had literally hired an engineer who was a brilliant engineer ...

> but he was not much help in picking material; he was a very indecisive guy, and that became a nightmare for us.

Rush's determination to move ever forward meant that they were suffering from their need to reinvent themselves, aiming to keep true to the meaning of the word 'progressive' in progressive rock. It would have been very easy – following what some saw as the misstep that was *Signals* – for the band to revert to the progressive and hard rock formula that had given them their big breakthrough, 1981's *Moving Pictures*. This was not the 'Rush Way'.

Grace Under Pressure was an apt title, reflecting both the mood of the new songs and the atmosphere in the studio. And, obviously, Henderson was not connected to the trio in the intrinsic way Terry Brown had been. The change in recording personnel from a familiar quartet to a trio plus a stranger meant that the usual ways of working were now out of the window. This rebalancing of relationships was akin to starting a new job. Eventually, after five months of gruelling, repetitive work, the record was completed. In *Chemistry*, Geddy recalled the pressure of the recording sessions:

> We had cabin fever by the end. You get to a dangerous state. You want to finish the record because you want to get out of there.

The cover matches the bleak contents and the crisp, sterile production. Syme's striking painting is an amalgam of details. Grace, denoted by the small 'g' on the right-hand side, is symbolised by a large body of calm water. Pressure (a lowercase 'p' above the 'g') is represented by rolling storm clouds. A granite-like section underneath the band name and the album title includes a jaw line of teeth and a bleeding gum line. A series of striations draws the attention to a small, bird-like eye staring out from the centre of the distant, crushing atmosphere. Three jagged shards of reflective metal are falling towards the water, and a silver-grey android-like figure observes all from the left-hand side.

The rear cover has a group portrait in black and white by famed photographer Yousef Karsh. The increasingly shorn Lifeson is doing his best 'boy next door' impression. Peart looks like someone a girl would definitely not want to take home to meet mother, whilst Lee is regrettably heading towards 'full mullet' status. A photograph on the lyric sleeve shows an egg held in an iron clamp. More grace, more pressure.

The album is a sonic improvement on *Signals*. There is a better balance between the guitars and the synths, there is space around the instruments and vocals, but it sounds and feels clinical. There is no acoustic guitar, nor any song which could be classified as a ballad. On the whole, the quality of the songwriting is somewhat higher than its predecessor, but conversely, there are no killer tracks of the stature of 'The Analog Kid' or 'New World Man' to raise the pulse, although 'Distant Early Warning', the best of the bunch, comes close. The stronger songs work well, but the overall feeling is one of engineered competence rather than passionate inspiration.

Peart's lyrics reflected the state of the world as he saw it, the lyricist largely taking his inspiration from newspapers of the day. Cold and realistic, at times downright dystopian, Peart still manages to convey a lot with an impressive economy. In *Chemistry*, the lyricist remembered:

> The mid-1980s were difficult times, economically, and people were losing jobs, having trouble getting work, having relationship problems and all that. The world looked dark.

'Distant Early Warning' (4.56)

The title takes its name from the Distant Early Warning Line, a series of radar stations stretching from Alaska to Greenland, the first notification point of a possible nuclear attack.

A rush of stormy synth, and suddenly the latest version of Rush is upon us. It's stripped back and, as promised, the synths share rather than suffocate the sound. Notably, Lifeson's Stratocaster is more prominent; the guitarist uses an overdriven tone to which lashings of reverb, delay and chorus effects (a sound modulation that approximates the chiming sound of a 12-string instrument) are added to varying degrees.

A brief, impressive section of spectacular proggery occurs at 28 seconds in; a simple church organ melody is added over four bars of 7/8, followed by single bars of 5/8 and 7/8. The music then settles down as Lee's almost conversational tone gives an unsettling context to some dark lyrics: An ill wind comes arising across the cities of the plain. There's no swimming in the heavy water, no singing in the acid rain – red alert!'

The second verse tightens the focus to examine personal relationships ('It's so hard to stay together passing through revolving doors'), culminating in a return of the prog organ motif, and – at last – a driving, energy-filled chorus where Lifeson takes his rightful place in the rocking mix.

The third and fourth verses maintain the tension, climaxing with the proggy organ tune, which moves into an even more powerful second chorus with some additional keyboard decoration. Then, Lifeson is let loose with some squealing, twisty phrases, mixed with upper-pitched chord voicings to produce an intriguing new style of solo, different to his flowing melodic lines we were accustomed to hearing on previous records. The final chorus concludes with an anguished-sounding Lee repeating 'Absalom'. As the last chord dies away, the sound of a desolate future landscape on a quiet synth is heard.

The strongest track on the album, 'Distant Early Warning' is also, along with 'Red Sector A' and 'Between The Wheels', one of the few tracks here to appear frequently on the band's subsequent live albums, which speaks volumes.

'Afterimage' (5.03)

A song written about the effects of a sudden death on those left behind, 'Afterimage' was inspired by the tragic loss of Le Studio recording assistant Robbie Whelan in a car crash in May 1983. He was only 31. This tribute to him is another lyrically powerful piece, but the music doesn't match the importance of the words.

The opening is full force, powerful and attacking, with Peart's excellent couplet ('Suddenly you were gone, from all the lives you left your mark upon') having an immediate resonance with anyone who has ever lost someone. Unfortunately, the power tails off as we return to the *Signals*-style ska rhythms for the verse, with the synth riding high in the mix.

The power builds in the next section ('I feel the way you would') with heartfelt, pain-filled phrases from Lifeson, who maintains his presence with some aggressive mid-range arpeggios. Again, Peart's words carry weight: 'Tried to believe but you know it's no good. This is something that just can't be understood'. Sadly, the ska style returns until a reprise of the 'I feel the way you would' section.

This leads into a lengthy synth-centric instrumental (2.23 – 3.45), which, whilst suitably melancholic, ultimately robs the song of much of its energy. Lifeson emerges from the sonic mush at 3.16 with another chord-based solo, which lifts interest, although his contribution is far from being his best work.

The coda of the song repeats the lyrics 'I feel the way you would, this just can't be understood' before coming to a close with a sustained synth chord that strangely just stops rather than fading away to nothing.

Given the intensely personal and yet universal theme, 'Afterimage' deserves to be a better song, either more reflective or much angrier in construction and delivery. The happy-sounding reggae rhythms that permeate much of the mood don't match the intent or weight of the lyrics.

'Red Sector A' (5.09)

Set in an unspecified prison camp in an unknown, possibly future time, Peart's words would carry an immense emotional weight for Lee, whose parents survived the Nazi concentration camps during the Second World War. In an interview with 'The Jewish News of Northern California' in June 2004, Geddy said:

> I once asked my mother her first thoughts upon being liberated. She didn't believe (liberation) was possible. She didn't believe that if there was a society outside the camp, how they could allow this to exist, so she believed society was done in.

Although the title could be the name of such a compound, or one in a major conflict yet to come, 'Red Sector A' was actually the name of the area where the band watched the Space Shuttle 'Columbia' take off, as documented in 'Countdown' (*Signals*).

Chiming guitars and sustained synth are supported by a rock-solid 4/4 rhythmic backing, with the absence of a time or a place emphasised in the opening stanza: 'All that we can do is just survive, all that we can do to help ourselves is stay alive'. This philosophy is neatly reflected in the song's closing lyrics: 'Are we the only ones left alive? Are we the only human beings to survive?'

A heavy synth riff takes over with splashes of guitar adding colour as the aggressive vocals create an oppressive texture to match the evocative words: 'Ragged lines of ragged grey, skeletons they shuffle away. Shouting guards and smoking guns will cut down the unlucky ones'. The perspective shifts to the personal with the harrowing lyrics: 'I clutch the wire fence until my fingers bleed, a wound that will not heal, a heart that cannot feel'. No doubt Geddy empathised with what Alex said in a radio interview on *Planet Rock* in April 2019:

> The first time I met Geddy's Mum, I saw her concentration camp number tattooed on her arm. That stayed with me. My parents came from Yugoslavia, and my father was in a work camp in Austria. The war affected everybody. Both my parents came to Canada as undocumented refugees. So Geddy and I shared a common background, and that really bonded us. Two Canadian-born Eastern Europeans whose parents had been displaced by the war.

What doesn't work so well here, again, is the counter-intuitive 'dance' feel of the electronic backing, which fails to synchronise emotionally with the lyrical intensity. Rather than the synth dominating the soundscape, this is surely the perfect opportunity for Lifeson to grind out some overdriven riffs to match the fear and pain within the narrator. These feelings are well portrayed by Lee's anguished vocals, none more so than with the couplet 'For my father and my brother it's too late, but I must help my mother stand up straight!'

Again, the busy, over-populated instrumental section sounds more like something that 'Frankie Goes To Hollywood' ('A mid-decade, electronic-based, popular beat combo, m'lud') would produce, with the prominence of sequencer and keyboard in the mix. Lifeson's 'new'-style solo unfortunately lacks the musical passion and expression to match the lyrical images. The song closes with more of the atmospheric instrumental section, concluding again with a fading synth.

'Red Sector A' is another example of Lifeson and Lee not stepping far enough up to Peart's lyrical plate. It's a good song, no doubt, but the definitive rendition can be heard on 2013's *Clockwork Angels Tour* triple CD live album. On this version, the throbbing synth, strident guitar and dramatic strings give this song a new maturity and edge with plenty of tension and dramatic colour. Additional elevation is provided by the presence of a string ensemble, adding a further layer to the tragedy of Peart's lyrics compared to the sterile, glacial tone of the original recording.

'The Enemy Within' (4.34)

Now we arrive at the first part of the 'Fear' trilogy. Whereas the previous two songs (the magnificent 'Witch Hunt' – confusingly subtitled, at the time, as 'Part 3 of 'Fear'' on *Moving Pictures* – and the disappointing and uneven 'The Weapon' on *Signals*, which was designated as 'Part Two' of the trilogy in reverse) had dealt with fears of external forces, here Peart is concerned with a person's paranoia, instilled by the various societal 'powers that be'.

The first 14 seconds of the introduction sound like Rush have abandoned their new sound in favour of a return to heavy rock. Then another rapid ska rhythm takes hold, with jagged, chorus-filled guitar stab chords. We are back in 'Vital Signs' territory, for better or worse.

Whilst the verses deal with many aspects of personal fear, the chorus is the first sighting of any lyrical optimism on the album. The music follows suit, adopting a 'New World Man'- style commitment, with energetic guitars, a full and thrusting bass and drums engaging the volume switch.

A short, dreamy instrumental (1.14 – 1.26) has a more relaxed feel and is, surprise, surprise, overwhelmingly synthy. Then, we're back into ska-mode for another unsettling verse and a rocking, upbeat chorus. The instrumental is extended (2.14 – 2.41), then the introduction is repeated.

The final minute and a half reprises the chorus, the instrumental and, finally, another ska-based race to the fading finish line. In the end, 'The Enemy Within' sounds like a collection of previously outcast musical ideas strung together to form a song that emits a strong odour of 'that will do'.

'The Body Electric' (4.59)

The title is taken from an episode of *The Twilight Zone* from 1962, which was itself based on Walt Whitman's poem 'I Sing The Body Electric'. Side two opens with a heavy, processed drum rhythm, a high-pitched bassline (the tone instantly placing the track in a mid-1980s time capsule) and then the by-now 'to-be-expected' blend of chorused, overdriven guitars and, of course, synth. The energy kicks in after 41 seconds before lapsing back for the unfolding of a tale describing 'one humanoid escapee, one android on the run, seeking freedom beneath a lonely desert sun'. Is there a place in the world for 'funk sci-fi'? Sci-funk? Discuss.

On the surface, this is an almost light-hearted story of a robot trying to break free of its programming. Is the robot seeking sentience, or are the lyrics to be interpreted as something more universal? 'It replays each of the days a hundred thousand years of routines ...' This may be a comment on our own existence, the balance between the need for routine and order and the abject boredom which comes from doing the same mind-numbing thing over and over again.

The chorus melody is catchy and powerful, and there is a frantic bridge section, which builds to a climax where the android 'bows its head and prays to the mother of all machines'. Step forward, Official Human Lifeson, to deliver another mixed bag of techniques for a solo, his whammy bar receiving much abuse. A reprised chorus and a repeat of the pacy, energetic section culminate in another 'mother of all machines' line. A play-out follows where no one instrument dominates, but all are fighting for space. Another power chord and a sustained synth fade ending bring the third good song on the album to a close.

'Kid Gloves' (4.18)
Another track with a 'New World Man' feel to it, 'Kid Gloves' opens with an excellent guitar riff in 5/4 time. This is carried over into the vocals, the song descending into another homage to The Police as the music drops into 4/4 at 40 seconds in. Peart observes the challenges of growing up in a world that is ripe for discovery – 'a world of difference, a world so out of touch. Overwhelmed by everything, but wanting more so much' – ending with the stylish line, 'Then you learn the lesson that it's cool to be so tough'. The chorus is one of the best sections on the album. The music drops in pitch, becoming heavier, with the synth adding much weight to the sound, this time in a good way.

The second verse (back into 5/4) continues the quality with 'a world of indifference, heads and hearts too full. Careless of the consequence, of constant push and pull'. Another heavied-up chorus appears, and then it's time for the sadly predictable-sounding instrumental.

Lifeson attacks his fretboard with gusto, but the creativity that marked out 'YYZ' and 'Limelight' (*Moving Pictures*) as solos of true inspiration and technical genius is absent. There's nothing actually wrong with what he plays, and, of course, in line with the band's mantra of always moving forward, he is doing a stellar job. It's just not to my taste, I guess.

In all other respects, 'Kid Gloves' is a standout track that comes to a hugely satisfying, heavy ending. Disappointingly, it would never feature on the band's live albums; it deserved better exposure.

'red lenses' (4.43)
The only Rush song that has its title solely in lowercase letters. The lyrics for all the songs are reproduced on the inner sleeve of the album, and for 'red lenses', they, too, are all shown in lowercase, with certain sections printed in red.

The most skippable track (not in the sense of a little jig) on the album, 'red lenses' bores both lyrically and musically. The words are merely a stream of consciousness that drones on around the word 'red', the music is unrelentingly mid-tempo and swamped by synth. A song that reeks of filler, the instrumental section is pure 1980s synth pomp-pop built around a repeating, irritating keyboard riff, which does at least have the good grace to grow into something more intense. However, this is neither interesting nor emotionally moving; it's just something that goes past the ears whilst you're doing something else.

In an interview for *Guitar For The Practising Musician* in October 1986, Peart acknowledged the influence of the poet T. S. Eliot (1888 – 1965) on his writing style.

> I can take someone like T.S. Eliot, who has influenced me greatly over the last few years, and realise that what he was doing was just throwing so many images at you all the time that you were left dizzy. But at the same time, you were left with something. You were stepping into another dimension. So I use that idea ... I tried to construct a series of ongoing images that just came at you. The colour red was the theme of it, but I twisted it in so many ways. It was the hardest thing I ever wrote, because I was trying not to say anything, and each line was saying something, but at the same time, it was trying to be so obscure and so oblique about the way I went around saying it, on purpose. It seems confounding, but in the end, you're left with something. T.S. Eliot's poetry is the same way to me. At the end of it, I don't really know what I've read, but it comes back to me.

Oh, good, that's alright then. What I'm left with is five wasted minutes for which no refund is available. Unsatisfying on every single level, 'red lenses' is stunningly underwhelming – a morass of poor ideas, lamely executed.

'Between The Wheels' (5.44)

Luckily, the final track of the record, which was also the first song to be written for the album, has a lot more going for it. From the strident organ chords, via the thunderous drumming, the mother of all guitar chords and anguished lead guitar lines, 'Between The Wheels' is powerful.

Lee rises to the challenge of the lyrics, his voice in a higher register at times. The pace picks up a minute in as we imagine 'how that rabbit feels, going under your spinning wheels, bright images flying by like windshields towards the fly'. The threat of nuclear war raises its head in the chorus, particularly with the final lines, 'Brother, can you spare – another war, another lost generation'.

'Between The Wheels' serves as a timely reminder that Rush, when they got bored with playing around with the then-fashionable music styles, could still deliver the goods in mighty style. The keyboards here sound menacingly foreboding, and they support rather than outweigh the attack of the guitar, bass and drums. Lifeson's solo cries out, the guitarist putting his heart into his fingertips, and adding much to this intense, passionate, groove-heavy rocker. Lee is in magnificent voice, and the play-out (which reprises the introduction) sounds huge.

Strangely, elements of an almost jazz-rock style improvisation appear as the music enters the fade, and this spoils the dramatic flow of the coda. The musical pressure should have been maintained right to the end.

Grace Under Pressure – Live (2009)

Personnel:
Alex Lifeson: electric and acoustic guitars
Geddy Lee: vocals, bass, synthesisers, bass pedals
Neil Peart: drums, percussion and electronic percussion
Recorded at Maple Leaf Gardens, Toronto, Ontario, Canada, on 21 September 1984
Released: 11 August 2009
Label: Mercury Records
Chart positions: did not chart

Initially, this live collection was only available as part of the triple DVD package, *Replay* (which contained the concert videos for *Exit – Stage Left*, *Grace Under Pressure Tour* and *A Show Of Hands*), which was released on 13 June 2006. The album was subsequently released as a CD in its own right three years later. It is an intriguing mixture of mostly recent and some older material.

With all the live albums reviewed in this volume, I have included comments only where individual points of interest arise. Rush's commitment to replicating their studio work on stage means that, with the many live albums between 1984 and 2015, there are inevitably a lot of songs that turn up again and again, and sound virtually identical to each other. What always shines through, however, is that the live band consistently sound better live than in the studio, which is quite the achievement.

Grace Under Pressure – Live is a case in point, showcasing powerful performances and instances of the band clearly enjoying themselves to an ecstatic crowd.

'Introduction' (0.57)
The theme of 'The Three Stooges' is heard above the sound of a very enthusiastic crowd.

'The Spirit Of Radio' (4.54)
'The Enemy Within' (4.48)

'The Weapon' (7.42)
We hear the sound effects of werewolves and demonic laughter, which sets up an amusing voice-over introduction by the American actor and comedian Joe Flaherty (1941 – 2024) in the guise of 'Count Floyd' over the relentless opening drum rhythm.

'Witch Hunt' (4.40)
'New World Man' (4.00)
'Distant Early Warning' (6.11)

'Red Sector A' (5.22)
Strangely, Geddy introduces this as 'We'd like to do another 'red' song for you'. Another? Has 'red lenses' made it onto the set-list? If so, I'm glad it didn't make the final cut onto this disc.

'Closer To The Heart' (3.36)

'YYZ'/'The Temples Of Syrinx'/'Tom Sawyer' (9.40)
The first time Rush truncated two songs into a mini-medley was 'Fly By Night'/'In The Mood' on *All The World's A Stage*. Here, it's only 'YYZ' that gets edited. After his solo, Lifeson continues to add phrases over the subsequent synth section, where the final chord is paused, and at 3.14, 'The Temples Of Syrinx' explodes out of the PA system. As with 'YYZ', the pace is slightly quicker than the studio version. Another slight pause at the end of all the metallic mightiness, and the trio plunge into 'Tom Sawyer' at 5.03, which is played at its familiar tempo.

'Vital Signs' (4.56)

'Finding My Way'/'In The Mood' (3.35)
This is a surprise inclusion for both the listener and the crowd. In the earliest days of Peart sitting in the drum seat, Rush would regularly play songs from their debut album for want of newer material. 'Working Man' would remain a semi-regular set-list staple, but the rest of the debut was, of course, quickly eclipsed by Lee, Lifeson and Peart's musical ambitions.

That said, the band sound like they are having genuine fun as they revitalise the opening track from their debut album. Sadly, the superior 'Finding My Way' is cut short after its first chorus and the trio move into the ever-lumpen 'In The Mood'. Although the reason for this song's inclusion never fails to perplex me, it is played with pace, attack and no sense of embarrassment.

Lee substitutes 'Hey Bully!' for 'Hey Baby!' in the choruses, which are both amusing and confusing, the song powering along into another mahoosive 'big rock' ending.

Power Windows (1985)

Personnel:
Alex Lifeson: electric and acoustic guitars
Geddy Lee: vocals, bass, synthesisers, bass pedals
Neil Peart: drums, percussion and electronic percussion
Synthesiser programming by Andy Richards and Jim Burgess
Additional keyboards by Andy Richards
Recorded at The Manor, England; Air Studios, Montserrat; and Sarm East, London, between April and August 1985
Produced by Peter Collins and Rush
Strings arranged and conducted by Anne Dudley, and recorded at Abbey Road Studios, London
Choir arranged and conducted by Andrew Jackman, and recorded at Angel Studios, London
Released: 26 October 1985
Label: Mercury Records
Chart positions: Canada: 2, US: 10, UK: 9
All music composed by Lee and Lifeson, with lyrics by Peart

A tour followed *Grace Under Pressure*, from May to November 1984, with the band playing in North America, Japan and Hawaii. The trio's collective mood, however, didn't match their commercial and critical success.

The collective finger was once again pointed at the now vacant producer's chair. It was felt that securing the right person at the helm would solve the problem. It couldn't be Terry Brown, and it wouldn't be Peter Henderson. A blend of experience and an objective ear was needed, someone tuned into the current musical thinking and capable of stepping back, giving detached opinions. The support act for part of the tour was noted blues rock guitarist Gary Moore, who suggested his own producer, Peter Collins.

Collins's CV already included 1980s pop stars Nik Kershaw, Tracy Ullman and Musical Youth. Not a natural fit, you might think, for the progressive rockers wanting to move with the influences of the period without compromising their core style. Collins was confident he could make the band sound better than his predecessors. The irony that Rush, who had determinedly fought against any form of outside direction or control, were now specifically seeking it seemed lost on the trio.

The band reassembled at the Elora Sound Studios in southern Ontario to write more music. As the material began to flow, an overarching lyrical theme of 'power' emerged as a link between the songs. *Grace Under Pressure* had focused on despair; the new project would project hope. The band and producer moved to the Manor Studios, with recording being relaxing and fulfilling.

In his autobiography, *My Effin Life,* Geddy expounded upon the attention to detail that Collins brought to the project:

> Rather than simply accepting the way we'd written a song, he'd ask us to try it in different keys or tempos. Sometimes, he'd suggest a reductive approach, breaking down a verse or a middle eight, eliminating certain instruments to make room for more dynamic parts to come. He believed strongly in injecting surges of energy as a song went along, either with a sound effect, guitar effect or keyboard flourish, arguing that a one-off event or a sudden change in feel will give a song longevity.

Vocals and overdubs were completed at Sarm East Studios. With the basic tracks finished, Collins suggested more innovations. Firstly, Andy Richards, who had played with Frankie Goes To Hollywood, Propaganda and Grace Jones, was employed as a specialist keyboard player. Lee, ever the perfectionist, felt he needed to offload some of the programming and playing to a musician whose first instrument was the keyboard. It was all very 1980s, all very glossy with plenty of reverb effect spread across every fader, all very 'un-Rush', as we thought we knew them. Real strings would feature on 'Manhattan Project' and 'Marathon'. A 30-piece orchestra and a 25-strong choir were duly engaged. Lifeson's guitars were completed at George Martin's Air Studios in Montserrat, with a month spent on mixing in England.

The cover is an intriguing piece by Syme. It's nighttime in an unwelcoming, darkened room. A teenage boy, one Neill Cunningham, wearing only pyjama bottoms, sits on a wooden chair. He is looking at us expressionlessly whilst pointing a remote control through a partially open, uncurtained window towards the out-of-view moon, the light from which illuminates the scene. The adolescent looks vaguely unhinged. On the bare wooden floorboards nearby sit three old television sets. Syme's theme is continued on the back cover with the same boy staring at us through a pair of binoculars. More windows with power, still semi-naked, still borderline psychopathic. The mood lifts slightly on the inner lyric sleeve with three individual colour photographs of the band, taken by the eminent Toronto photographer Dimo Safari. Against black backgrounds, Alex is smiling with arms crossed, Neil ... isn't, while Geddy's dark hair and jacket mean very little of him is actually visible. At least the mullet appears to be in retreat.

Over-produced, overdubbed to astonishing levels and polished to within an inch of whatever life some of the songs started out with, *Power Windows* sees Rush happy to be engulfed by everything that keyboard technology could offer. In their latest producer, the band had found someone completely disinterested in their past, a person in sync with the prevailing musical trends and the cutting-edge technology needed to realise such sounds.

The chief problem with *Power Windows* is that it sticks so very closely to the template it quickly establishes. There is little space for effective dynamics, 'Manhattan Project' excepted, and all the songs come in between five and six-and-a-half minutes. There are no shorter, snappier songs to break up the feel of lengthy repetition. Similarly, there's little difference between each track's sonic style, with similar tempos employed throughout. It's the combined and constant assault on the eardrums, which proves wearing after repeated listens. Only three of the eight tracks remain effectively in the memory. That's not a good return on the listener's investment.

That said, in *Limelight – Rush In The '80s*, Neil praised the band's effort:

> *Power Windows* really hangs together well as a whole body of work, I think, the way it's shaped. Running order is something we've always spent a lot of time and debate on. And I think it's a great running order on this; from top to bottom, I think it's a really good performance.

In *Rush – Beyond The Lighted Stage*, he said:

> We all loved the music of that time, we were young enough to, and we didn't have any protective nature of what Rush was, that it could never be allowed to be influenced by New Wave music, or could never use an African rhythm. There was no such thing as 'That doesn't suit Rush'; those words have never been uttered.

Entering into the 'synth/guitar' debate, Alex said:

> I loved the idea of the keyboards when we first started. I think that as that part of our sound developed, there were times where we just got on the wrong track.
>
> With *Power Windows* I found it really, really difficult to work around the way the keyboards were developing. Why am I looking for a different place? I shouldn't be looking for a different place. What's going on with these keyboards? You know, there're not even real, not even a real instrument!

Geddy added his perspective:

> Alex and I had some real disagreements about how profound the keyboards should be, but 'Power Windows' is a really important record because it was the final and essential blending of keyboards and guitar to me for Rush.

Power Windows does have its devotees. When 'The Big Money', 'Marathon' and 'Grand Designs' appeared on subsequent live albums, they sounded good. Not brilliant, but certainly better. However, as noted Rush fan and McFly main man Tom Fletcher might well ask, 'Where did all the guitars go?' Despite the remarkable demonstration of keyboard sounds, only three of its eight songs made it to official live status. This collection felt, at the time, like the nadir of the band's 1980s output. Today, I feel the same way about it. You need to know it gives me no pleasure in writing that.

'The Big Money' (5.34)

A record's producer is as integral to a song's success as the ideas contained in the initial writing. Put another way, the fact that 'A Farewell To Kings' and 'Moving Pictures' are such great albums is in no small part due to the input and skills of Terry Brown. In a similar way, 'The Big Money' is the best song on *Power Windows* despite the involvement of Peter Collins.

First impressions? The sound is bright, full, swamped with reverb, and there's a lot going on in the background. The lyrics are more a list than a narrative; Peart considers the power of those with vast amounts of money for both good and evil, coming down on neither side except with the final lines, 'Big money got a mean streak, big money got no soul', during which Lee excels vocally. In an interview with *The Boston Globe* in 1985, Peart said:

> I didn't want the song to be totally in the voice of a cynical, anti-corporate reactionary, though, because things like the Ford Foundation do accomplish a lot of good. I mean, the church and worthy events like Live Aid are big money, too.

'The Big Money' is an excellent opener; brisk, busy and intense, there is still plenty to be admired amongst all the glossy, shiny sounds. The introduction is powerful with guitar chords in seeming battle with the keyboards, followed by a bouncy 'all synth and sound effects' section before the song moves up a notch with the vocals. Behind all the technical sonic wizardry, the trio's instrumental skills are on full display; Lifeson plays plenty of interesting, energised chordal contributions, there is a very fast and aggressive bassline throughout and Peart keeps things lively in the reverb-heavy background.

There is also plenty of melody in evidence, especially with the 'It's the power and glory ... on a tumble of a dice' section (1.30 – 1.40). Full of energy and brimming with confidence, even all the synths can't subdue the track's spirit here, especially when Lifeson's magnificent chord progression shines out at 2.33.

The play out is fantastic. The introduction is repeated, the music seemingly coming to rest, then Lifeson steps forward and hammers out the descending chord sequence in 6/4 time as Peart attacks his kit with venom. This fades away quickly, which is a shame, as this section could have done with further development.

'Grand Designs' (5.05)

Another song which, like 'The Big Money', takes its title from a Don Passos publication, 'Grand Designs' is about the power of the mind, of ideas, for good or ill. Starting promisingly with a classy uber-prog keyboard ostinato punctuated with powerful chords and drum fills, regrettably, the song then slips into the ska stylings that spoiled some of the tracks on the previous two albums. Lyrically, the song is a critique of conformity. We are urged to go 'against the run of the mill', to 'swim against the stream', otherwise we will exist 'in two dimensions' as part of 'a mass production scheme'.

Putting their rock trousers back on, Rush build up the power with the next section – 'Like a rare and precious metal ... a lot of useless talk' – before reprising the introduction, which is the best part of the composition. 'Grand Designs' oscillates around these three ideas continually. Lifeson's guitars stab and crisply strum, and his solo (2.55 – 3.21) has some inventive ideas combined with a searing, sustained tone, which continues into Lee's final vocal section.

The song continues with a multi-tracked, sing-along melody over a vigorous rhythm section. The introduction is reprised with Peart giving it his all in the syncopated stabs department. The band intended a quick fade at this point, but because of Peart's masterful playing, the music was allowed to continue and then eventually disappear.

'Manhattan Project' (5.05)

Concerning the secret American project to develop a nuclear bomb with a view to bringing World War 2 to an end, 'Manhattan Project' is also interesting for its lack of guitar and bass in significant sections of the song. For the first and third verses, the instrumentation is made up of just vocals, keyboards and drums. The change is a welcome contrast to the aural bombardment we have endured thus far.

The song begins with an ominous synth simulating the sound of a bomber; military drums and a punchy bass add to the tension, but when the keyboards and guitar join in, the mood suddenly becomes warm and summery, which might be considered unsuitable for the subject matter.

Unusually for a song written about a possible nuclear war, Peart resists the temptation to take sides. Neither for nor against, he merely observes and passes comment with the detached quality of a historian. The lyrics have an intimate, curious quality: 'Imagine a time when it all began, in the dying days of a war, a weapon that would settle the score'. Peart crystallises the lessons of history well: 'Whoever found it first would be sure to do their worst. They always had before'.

The second verse, with added bass and isolated, scattering guitar runs, considers the minds of the men who devised the device. The point is obliquely made that research was being carried out by both sides in the conflict.

At 1.23, Lifeson is more clearly heard with a cleanly picked arpeggio riff. The atmosphere builds and the rhythm section kick in with purpose for 'the big bang, took and shook the world, shot down the rising sun'. This is a highlight of the song, the story being told in poetic detail, written with intelligence and sung with conviction.

When the musical mood lightens for the third verse, it feels counterintuitive. At various points (0.52 and 1.21, for example), the heavy synth chords sound appropriately threatening. Here, in 'a place where it all began ... in the secrecy of the desert sand', the sound is less menacing and more carefree. A repeated chorus builds into the dramatic final verse. A sudden break in the music under Lee's high-pitched 'flying out of the shock-wave' is especially effective, leaving the impression of a pilot flying away from the destruction he has been ordered to unleash. The last words are the most prophetic: 'All the powers that be, and the course of history, would be changed forevermore'. The two nuclear attacks on Japan effectively ended the Pacific phase of the Second World War. Unfortunately, the threat of nuclear obliteration is still a possibility, rather than a memory.

At 3.21, the orchestral musicians appear with an agitated ostinato over which a soaring violin melody is added, blending with an inappropriate chiming guitar. The chorus is reprised, and then a brief, pained guitar solo brings this impressive work to a close, the music fading out with a reprise of the introduction.

In an interview with *Blender* magazine Geddy spoke of the production opportunities and ideas which were utilised in this epic composition:

> We pulled things out, but tried never to lose the focus of the trio. In 'Manhattan Project', on verse one and verse three, it's vocals, drums and keyboards. This is not a typical thing for this band. Let's pull the bass and guitar out? How can you do this to a Rush song? But it worked, and I loved the effect of it.

Good though 'Manhattan Project' is, it would have been better served by the dystopian production of *Grace Under Pressure*. Or, you can 'imagine a time' when it would have been produced by Terry Brown ...

'Marathon' (6.09)

A steady, relentless guitar, bass and drum introduction soon gives way to a double-time tempo with a spectacularly quick and funky bassline. Writing neither about the historical battle in Greece nor the equally legendary chocolate bar, the lyrics are a metaphor for life itself, with endurance as its central point.

The chorus is the highlight of the track. Melodic, uplifting and memorable, it is backed by a wall of celebratory-sounding synths, and Lee's vocals work particularly well here, evoking the pride and joy that comes from successfully completing an endeavour; the harder the task, the greater the satisfaction.

After the second appearance of the chorus, the band move into an excellent instrumental section. This is set against a tense 7/8 time signature. Bass and drums set up the initial jerky riff with Lifeson adding single sustained notes, layer upon layer, to create an ethereal effect. This is soon destroyed when he plays the riff at a lower pitch with a great distorted tone. This sound moves upstage as the synths storm in with long chords over the continuing rhythm, then the guitarist throws in a chaotic-sounding, yet carefully crafted, solo.

The song's theme is driven home with the synth-heavy mid-section at 4.16: 'You can do a lot in a lifetime if you don't burn out too fast.' The 7/8 rhythm then reappears with more layers of Lifeson before breaking out into repeats of the chorus, as the finishing line hovers into view. Strings are added to the fade as this impressive track disappears into the distance. The fade may be intentionally aligned with the lyrical themes; you never actually finish the race, you just keep going until you can run no more.

'Territories' (6.19)

The song's title was inspired by the New Territories area near Hong Kong. Chinese influences abound in the spacious and dreamlike introduction. It's not difficult to imagine this as the musical backing for a film encouraging tourism to the country.

The lyrics for 'Territories' were written after Peart visited China for the first time. The opening line referencing the Middle Kingdom ('I see the Middle Kingdom between Heaven and Earth') is what China calls itself today. The reason for the Middle Kingdom is that it's slightly below Heaven, but still above everybody on Earth.

The words, rather than focusing on any particular nation, offer up a savage criticism of propaganda and the nationalistic tendencies of any country. This parallels his stance in 'Grand Designs'; borders have no effect on man's capacity for the extremes of positive or negative outcomes in life. One country is as capable of inflicting hardship as another. After all, one man's terrorist is another's freedom fighter. It's all down to your point of view and the circumstances of your birth in the end. Whilst this is all good and worthy, yet again the power of his writing is unsuitably supported by a wall of glossy effects and soft focus synths.

As if in response to this, there are moments when Lifeson comes alive and unleashes some suitably angry riffage. Immediately, words, music and vocals fall into sync, and the song works. Unfortunately, 'Territories' suffers from a case of too many instruments spoiling the listener's appreciation of the excellent lyrical content. In the background, it's all synth-on-synth action and busy drumming. The relative lack of dynamics, the all-pervading keyboards and the unfaltering tempo instil a kind of numbness; there is very little of distinctive quality standing out amidst everything else that's going on.

'Middletown Dreams' (5.15)

This opens with another film soundtrack-like introduction. Predictable instrumentation, a mundane, unrelenting tempo and a vocal melody line that redefines the word 'dull', 'Middletown Dreams' manages to disappoint on every level.

Whether it is the office worker with a drink problem, the awkward teenager or the middle-aged housewife painter, all of them, Peart tells us, dream of changing their lives. Do they? By the time the chorus has arrived, the lyricist sounds like a motivational poster that has achieved sentience: 'Dreams flow across the heartland feeding on the fires. Dreams transport desires, drive you when you're down. Dreams transport the ones who need to get out of town'. Do they? Okay, whatever you say ...

Such platitudes may be forgiven if the accompanying music showed signs of innovation, creativity or the passion required to pursue such an ambition. Sadly, it has none of these attributes. By now, we know what to expect, and this song duly delivers it in spades. Everything sounds like we've heard it before ... because we have. If the idea was to represent the potentially tedious repetition of everyday life in musical form, it succeeds magnificently. There are no distinguishing features; Lifeson's solo sounds like he is venting his frustration at playing a subjugated role in the band, and when he is let off the leash, it all comes pouring out. In comparison, Lee's vocal melody sounds uninspired and perhaps recorded with a view to coming up with something better later.

'Emotion Detector' (5.10)

Initially slow to the point of ponderous, 'Emotion Detector' is as unpersuasive as its title. Despite being about the power of relationships, this ends up being yet another mid-tempo track with shiny sonic busyness going on everywhere, possibly designed to distract from the lack of anything interesting to focus on in the main body of the song. Ironically, 'Emotion Detector' sounds like the soundtrack to a loveless marriage, a chore, a routine, just to pass the time.

The chorus is the most engaging part, with Peart commenting on the extremes of optimism and the cynicism of despair, which can characterise many relationships. Musically, this is another egregious example of Rush's take on synth pop-rock, another long five-minute song that bores and frustrates in equal measure. By now, Lifeson's solo sound is beginning to grate on the ears. His solo sounds so similar here to his other contributions that it suggests it may have been simply transplanted from a discarded take of an earlier track.

'Mystic Rhythms' (5.53)

If anyone was hoping for a stirring finale with the emotional heft of 'The Big Money', 'Manhattan Project' or 'Marathon', they were in for yet another disappointment. It's not the band's desire to keep step with technological improvements that irks me; it's the monumental dullness of these last four songs which sticks in my craw, wherever that is.

So, what do we get? Lots of drums of different sounds and persuasions? Check. Dreamy, ambient synths? Of course. Chiming, chorused guitar motifs? Naturally. An uninspiring vocal melody that fails to engage heart or mind? Big tick. The lyrics ask us to wonder at the intense diversity of the universe. There may be powers out there far greater than us, whose presence and purpose we may only vaguely glimpse in our peripheral vision. If so, I hope they can write better music than this in their honour.

The most musically involving part is again the chorus. Once that's out of the way, it all drags; backwards guitars, sampled drums and a sense of 'when it will stop', rather than a sense of wonder at the universe. 'Mystic Rhythms' eventually fades away. The music lacks the emotional power, sense of wonder or desire to explore and learn that the lyrics suggest. But this is, of course, merely my opinion.

In *Contents Under Pressure*, Neil opined on the album:

> That's one I particularly like. If you try to divorce yourself from musician to fan, I think – as a fan – I would particularly like those records (*Power Windows* and *Hold Your Fire*) just because they are such a feast to listen to – so much texture and so much variety and rhythmic exploration. To me, they remain very satisfying pieces of work to listen to. So I think that's about the highest tribute I can give it; they are something I would like as a fan.

Hold Your Fire (1987)

Personnel:
Alex Lifeson: electric and acoustic guitars
Geddy Lee: vocals, bass, synthesisers, bass pedals
Neil Peart: drums, percussion and electronic percussion
Arrangements by Rush and Peter Collins
Synthesiser programming by Andy Richards and Jim Burgess
Additional keyboards by Andy Richards
Additional vocals by Aimee Mann
Strings arranged and conducted by Stephen Margoshes
The William Farey Engineering Brass band arranged and conducted by Andrew Jackman; recorded at Mirage Studios, Oldham, England
Recorded at The Manor, Oxfordshire; Ridge Farm Studios, Surrey; Air Studios, Montserrat; McClear Place, Toronto; and the Lerxst Mobile between 5 January and 24 April 1987
Mixed at Studio Guillaume Tell, Suresnes, Paris
Produced by Peter Collins and Rush
Released: 8 September 1987
Label: Mercury Records
Chart positions: Canada: 9, US: 13, UK: 10
All music composed by Lee & Lifeson, with lyrics by Peart, except 'Force Ten' by Peart and Dubois

Power Windows had gone Gold by Christmas 1985 and Platinum the following month. A subsequent tour of North America began in December 1985, lasting through to March 1986.

The band had enjoyed the *Power Windows* experience, and Collins was retained for the next album. Writing commenced in September 1986, with Peart developing a theme in his lyrics, which Geddy summed up in *Chemistry*:

> It relates to the burning desire to do something and how important it is to keep your fire lit, regardless of circumstances. It's important to hold yourself together, to stick to your guns. What we've been striving to achieve over the last three or four records has finally come to rest with *Hold Your Fire*. We climbed up a hill, and now we've gotten to the top, and we have to decide where we go from here.

The songs were studio-ready by the end of the year, and in January 1987, recording commenced back in England. Both producer and band wanted to push sonic possibilities and boundaries. This meant exploring further the opportunities of the ever-developing keyboard and recording technology, whilst incorporating new percussive textures suitable to the musical landscapes the band wanted to explore.

The album appeared almost two years after *Power Windows. Hold Your Fire* took full advantage of a CD's increased maximum duration. Rush's 12th studio album was their longest so far, clocking in at just over 50 minutes, split over ten songs. There's a lot of music to get into. Time well spent? We shall see.

The front cover was their most understated to date. Overwhelmingly red, a triangle of three red globes floats above a red surface upon which the balls cast their shadows. This minimalist design was in stark contrast to Syme's inner gatefold picture, which was originally intended for the front cover. The incredibly detailed image, showing a mocked-up city street scene at night, is another pun-fest constructed by Peart and Syme. On the rear of the, yet again, red sleeve, we have three sepia-toned individual portraits. From top to bottom, Lifeson has just washed his floppy blonde locks, Peart's hair appears to be leaving his head on a vertical trajectory and it is sad to note that Lee has now gone full ponytail.

Hold Your Fire is a sonic sequel to *Power Windows*, although the album's lyrical themes are different. For a band so wedded to the idea of change and progress, these two records sound like two very similar sides of the same shiny coin. Both contain a huge variety of keyboard sounds and percussion textures, both demonstrate a desire to incorporate the popular musical styles of the time, and both address serious lyrical ideas.

To my ears, the pop-centric production, the overbearing use of synthesisers and Lifeson's reduced role in the face of the overwhelming advances in keyboard technology mean that this pair of releases is not 'closer to my heart'. Rush, of course, wanted to always progress and break new sonic ground. Hence, the inclusion of a brass band, orchestral string players on 'Mission', 'High Water' and 'Second Nature' and a gospel choir on the final section of 'Prime Mover'.

Speaking of the album overall, in *Beyond The Lighted Stage*, Geddy said:

> *Hold Your Fire* was the record that told me that there was a shift in the way we were writing that was pushing us away from rock. We were starting to move into a jazzier, softer kind of tonal area.

Alex:

> *Hold Your Fire* was a good record. We were sort of coming to the end of our foray into the world of keyboards. *Power Windows* was so layered with keyboards, and *Hold Your Fire* was a bit of a relief; we kind of pulled back a little bit on the use of keyboards. But it was part of the '80s thing; that was the sort of headspace we were at then.'

'Force Ten' (4.31)

That said, things get off to a good start with this fast-paced, driving rocker that was a last-minute addition to the recording schedule, quickly fashioned around a recently completed lyric, itself inspired by some lines written by Pye Dubois, who would occasionally send some of his work to Peart to see if it was of interest.

While 'Force Ten' is no 'Tom Sawyer', it is a decent enough opener and the band sound alive, if very comfortable within the smooth confines of this slickly produced album. After an unconventional start involving a choir, a cheering crowd, a distorted guitar chord, a pneumatic drill and a woman's laughter, drums fade in with a pulsing rhythm, the bass kicks with a driving riff and Lifeson attacks with gusto.

My first gripe is with the opening lines: 'Tough times ... demand tough songs' may be true, but this isn't one of them. The lyrics concern life's pressures and how we respond to them. Consequently, the music should possess a greater tension than it does. There should be stress, drive, some angst to the instrumentation; a distorted guitar that is mixed to land right between the eyes, backed by a ferocious bass and pulverising percussion. Sadly, the sonic effect is more like being driven in an expensive, well-appointed SUV with electronic everything and comfort to spare, as it effortlessly cruises down a motorway at speed. Whilst the tempo is hypnotic, and the vocal melody memorable, there is a real sense that underneath all the studio's luxurious soft furnishings, Rush really want to rock.

A more reflective and melodic, synth-backed section emerges at 1.23 ('Look into the eye of the storm ...') before the main riff kicks back in with proper attitude. Some spectacular synth arpeggios illuminate the backing before the return of the synth chorus at 2.34. These two sections intermingle throughout the song, until the opening words are repeated and an assault of sampled drums brings things to a tight end.

'Time Stand Still' (5.09)

The first song written for the album is another cracker, with a catchy, commercial edge to it. 'Time Stand Still' keeps the spirits lifted with its foot-tapping tempo, crisp, chorused guitar work and evocative lyrics.

The first verse extends the 'weather-as-life' metaphor of 'Force Ten'. In an interview with the *Boston Globe* in November 1987, Neil said:

> All through the 1970s, our lives were flying by; we spent so much time on the road that it became like a dark tunnel. You start to think about the people you are neglecting, friends and family. So the song is about stopping to enjoy that, with a warning against too much looking back. Instead of getting nostalgic about the past, it's more of a plea for the present.

Come the chorus, the mood becomes more reflective as the song's title is sung by Aimee Mann, vocalist with new wave band 'Til Tuesday, her soft, reassuring voice interweaving with Lee's response phrases. This is the first time anybody outside of the band has sung on a Rush song, and Mann's appearances are a surprising and refreshing addition to the sound. In a promotional interview from 1988, Geddy said:

> We knew that the part she sang was a feminine part. We didn't want to use a keyboard or have Alex or me sing it, so we started looking for a female singer. It's a very attractive opportunity for us to work with a female singer. We just looked until we found a voice that was suitable. In listening to Aimee's last record, we loved the way she sang, so we just asked her.

In another interview promoting the new album, Neil reflected upon the song title and lyrics:

> My first idea was to write about time, and the first song I wrote was 'Time Stand Still'. But the more I thought about it and played around with the ideas, the more the expanded idea of temperamental barriers took shape. 'Time Stand Still' applies to that concept in that it deals with the attitude of enjoying life and not letting it whisk by without appreciating it.

Moving effortlessly between 7/4 in the guitar introduction – made up of a repeated guitar melody and ghostly, swirling synths – and a steadily grooving 4/4 (for the rest of the track), 'Time Stand Still' grows in intensity. Peart saves his best lyrics for the final verse – a reflection on the nature of the passing of time, and how it seems to speed up as we grow older: 'Summer's going fast, nights growing colder, children growing up, old friends growing older, experience slips away' – before this excellent song closes as it began, with chorused guitar arpeggios.

'Open Secret' (5.38)
The ghost of *Power Windows* raises its head with this synth-heavy, mid-tempo track that lacks the drive or melodicism of the two preceding songs. The lyrics centre on conflict and communication in personal relationships, and the inherent problem of what might happen were we to be totally honest with one another, as opposed to the safe but solitary option of keeping secrets safely hidden.

Behind the vocals, however, this is mediocre music played without spirit or flair. Things dip lower still in the softer section after the second chorus. Here, Peart becomes clunky: 'You could try to understand me; I could try to understand you'. It's like a counselling session set to spa music.

Lifeson then enters the room with a squealing, busy solo, which is the most involving part of this mundane composition. The central motif is repeated and the music resumes cruise control as it glides away to a close.

'Second Nature' (4.36)
A gentle electric piano introduction and subtle hi-hat indicate a significant change of pace and mood. 'Second Nature' is a sort of follow-up to 'Closer To The Heart' from a decade ago, in that Man's ability for goodness lies within

himself, but a degree of compromise is essential for any desired change to come about: 'A memo to a higher office, open letter to the powers that be'. Rock, and indeed, roll.

The chorus ('It ought to be second nature ...') keeps the melodic content high, the texture building subtly with increased instrumentation. Chiming guitar and the full rhythm section crash in supporting the wordplay: 'I know you're different, you know I'm the same, we're both too busy to be taking the blame'. It's this change of dynamics that makes 'Second Nature' an effective, thought-provoking piece.

The second verse succinctly summarises life: 'Folks are basically decent, conventional wisdom would say. Well, we read about the exceptions in the papers everyday'. This is quickly followed by the magnificently full sound of another chorus, expansive and powerful.

A synth-led, heavy instrumental section precedes another powerful chorus, the song ending without a resolution to the paradox posed: our lives are too busy, too pressured for us to take the time out to rework how we should live, thereby improving the quality of existence. 'Second Nature' is another good, but not great, addition to the Rush canon.

'Prime Mover' (5.19)

Peart's voracious appetite for literature is further demonstrated as he expands upon Greek philosopher Aristotle's view that the universe must possess a prime mover, a power, or presence that is responsible for all activity within it. The purpose of any living thing with free will is unknown until tested. Weighty stuff indeed, especially when contrasted with the upbeat pop-rock synth music accompanying the words.

An energetic opening, full of bright guitars and synths, gives way to a quieter verse where Lifeson has a repeating melody, similar to the one deployed in 'The Weapon' (*Signals*) – vaguely Celtic and very tasty.

'Prime Mover' is a catchy, tuneful chugger that is, at times, satisfyingly heavy; the various sections keep the song interesting both lyrically and musically, and these succeed in conveying the optimistic interpretation of the 'anything can happen' refrain.

'Lock And Key' (5.09)

A dramatic church organ sound ushers in the opening lines: 'I don't want to face the killer instinct, face it in you or me'. This is a song about everyone's 'dark side', and the struggle to keep it under control. Peart acknowledges that anger can be unleashed with both positive and negative outcomes. Finding a balance is integral for survival, as beneath it all, we all possess 'the heart of a lonely hunter' who 'guards a dangerous frontier'. As with 'Force Ten', the concept is well thought out, but it is executed within such a comfortable musical setting as to render much of its intended power largely impotent.

Luckily, Lifeson is on hand to dish out some much-needed dirt, and there's plenty of melody bouncing around the composition. Lifeson pours heart and soul into some serious fretboard and whammy bar work; he is eventually left spent, and we're lying back in the warm afterglow of more choruses, more synths, more sameness. Lee's repetition of the opening lines sounds increasingly laboured and inauthentic. At least there's a decent hard rock build-up to the song's close, with Peart going crazy on his kit, as the track fades away. It would have sounded better with a definitive ending.

'Mission' (5.16)

In *Contents Under Pressure*, Geddy said:

> The song 'Mission' is really a song I'm proud of in terms of melody and a kind of boldness, taking it in the direction we did. That record was influenced a lot by Peter Collins in the sense that his love of melody and what we'd gone through on *Power Windows* was still resonating with us. Some of those were very, very difficult songs to put together texturally.

With another sustained, soothing synthesiser opening and another warm bath of sound, we're back in the world of the motivational speaker: 'Hold your fire, keep it burning bright, hold the flame 'til the dream ignites. A spirit with a vision is a dream with a mission'. Posters with silhouettes of eagles flying into sunsets over mountain ranges spring to mind.

Fortunately, things move up several gears 26 seconds in with more pulsing synth pop-rock, which at least has the decency to feature plenty of guitars. For most of its duration, 'Mission' just cruises along; whilst pretty in places, it is lyrically uninspiring.

However, the ears prick up for the instrumental (2.48 – 3.41). Out of the routine appears something rather special. A guitar ostinato in 5/4 time explodes into some aggressive lead guitar pyrotechnics, and, bizarrely, a brief bass and glockenspiel solo. No, really. Then some stupendously heavy guitar work reminds you that Rush really can deliver when they choose to. Take away the cave-like reverb from the mix, and this section is an overwhelming, if too short, display of awesome musical power.

The mood calms dramatically for a soft synth sequence that reflects on the 'cold comfort to the ones without it, to know how they've struggled, how they've suffered about it'. The music returns to its previous heroic, if overproduced, texture with the repeated blandishments of 'A spirit with a vision is a dream with a mission'. The final seconds are saved by another highly emotive Lifeson solo, which fades away too soon.

'Turn The Page' (4.55)

A lively bass riff in 6/4 time is joined by guitars, synth and drums in this pacy rocker that studies our reactions to whatever disaster befalls an area of the world away from our own. Not knowing the sufferers personally doesn't mean we are unaffected by the events, but it's too easy for us to move on and 'turn the page'.

The verse is played out in long phrases of three bars of 4/4 time, which makes the music sound 'proggier' than it actually is. The chorus falls into a half-time tempo with the appearance of the church organ synth, which is soon joined by modulation-enhanced guitars. The driving rhythm boosts the energy into the second verse.

The bass introduction is reprised, leading into one of those 'How come he doesn't break a string?' guitar solos, such is the intensity and attack of Lifeson's string-bending technique. Playing like a maniac, he throws everything he's got at the track. His solo is a screaming, painful and impressive demonstration of what a guitar can convey. High energy and even more highly produced choruses bring the track to an end.

'Tai Shan' (4.15)

In complete contrast, 'Tai Shan' is a beautifully evocative melodic ballad where, finally, the synths are more welcome to the ears than the overly bright bite of the guitar arpeggios.

We are back in China, specifically, the farthest east of the country's five greatest mountains. 'Tai Shan' is both a place of worship and an important ceremonial location, and Peart felt a sense of wonder when he visited the place whilst cycling in the region: 'In the golden light of Autumn, there was magic in the air'. With just a few well-chosen words, the lyricist puts us in his place.

Musically, the song has a calm, other-worldly quality that doesn't require Lifeson's guitar prowess, unless a gentle acoustic guitar was added for extra texture. The combination of strong melodies and an emotive vocal performance with keyboard support and the understated percussive rhythms would be enough. The chorus is excellent, simple and relatively unadorned. It makes its point without, for once in this 'Collins Era', overdoing it. Sometimes, less is genuinely more.

'High Water' (5.33)

'High Water' is yet another over-laden, mid-tempo track with few redeeming features. The chorus, however, is melodic, and the verse immediately following it is full of overdriven electric guitar playing a chord sequence that is vaguely reminiscent of the mood of 'Bacchus Plateau' (*Caress Of Steel*). Lifeson has another opportunity to shine with a sinewy solo and some intense, interweaving phrases in the final chorus. Whilst 'Storm Force Ten' was an effective opener with plenty of promise, 'High Water' fails to bring the album to a similarly satisfying conclusion.

In *Contents Under Pressure*, Geddy expressed a fondness for the album:

> It's a very ambitious piece, full of textural changes, dramatic, rhythmic changes. And it's quite a romantic album in some ways.

A Show Of Hands (1989)

Personnel:
Geddy Lee: bass guitar, synthesisers, vocals
Alex Lifeson: guitars, synthesisers, backing vocals
Neil Peart: acoustic and electronic percussion
Recorded at Le Mobile and Advison Mobile between 1986 and 1988
Engineered by Guy Charbonneau
Mixed at McClear Place Studios, Toronto
Released on 9 January 1989
Label: Mercury Records
Chart positions: Canada: did not chart, US: 21, UK: 12
All music composed by Lee & Lifeson, with lyrics by Peart, except 'The Rhythm Method', music by Peart

Rush continued with the precedent of issuing a live album after every four studio releases. *All The World's A Stage* (1976) had been youthfully raw and urgent, whilst 1981's *Exit Stage Left* succeeded in showcasing much of the band's best material to date but suffered from too much studio tinkering in an attempt to present the 'perfect' live album. *A Show Of Hands* manages to strike a balance between the two, and again acted as a shop window for much of the content of their 'synth era'. The album succeeds in capturing the power of live performance with a clarity of production; all the songs presented here sound better than their studio counterparts.

Hold Your Fire was the last album of this period for the band. A subsequent tour, from October 1987 to May 1988, included Europe for the first time since *Signals*, with the technical demands of reproducing the recent material live proving problematic. 'Witch Hunt', which had originally been recorded purely as a studio song with no thoughts of a live performance, could now be played effectively on stage, but the heavier keyboard textures of 'Power Windows' proved a step too far, with occasional breakdowns or programming errors.

Once away from the tour, the band recognised that the keyboards had overtaken their core sound, and to a large extent, outstayed their welcome. A paring back and refocusing were necessary, and in some minds, long overdue. With *A Show Of Hands*, the guitar resumes a more prominent role in the mix and, whilst it confines itself in the main to only a single decade, the material is well presented and performed with the band's customary conviction.

The concert dates recorded in Birmingham, United Kingdom, were considered the best for a third double live album with six tracks ('Turn The Page', 'Manhattan Project', 'Mission', 'Mystic Rhythms', 'Witch Hunt' and 'Force Ten') culled from performances across America. Only 'Mystic Rhythms' and 'Witch Hunt' were taken from dates on the *Power Windows* tour. Drawing almost exclusively from *Signals* onwards, the album also completed and subsequently freed Rush from their contract with Mercury.

The band released a video version of the album with a DVD following in 2006. These formats included additional songs – 'Prime Mover', 'Territories', 'The Spirit Of Radio', 'Tom Sawyer' – and an encore medley of '2112', 'La Villa Strangiato' and, yet again, 'In The Mood'.

In *Contents Under Pressure*, Geddy said:

> *A Show Of Hands* to me is a very fine album. That style of recording a live album, basically taking a handful of shows and choosing the best you've got ... to me, that is a very good representation of that kind of live album. In terms of the construction of it, I think it was down to Paul Northfield and me, mostly.

'Introduction' (0.53)
Again, the band's sense of humour is on display with the cartoony introductory music (the theme from 'The Three Stooges'), which includes 'Three Blind Mice', naturally.

'The Big Money' (5.59)
'Subdivisions' (5.22)
'Marathon' (6.32)
'Turn The Page' (4.41)
'Manhattan Project' (5.18)
'Mission' (5.46)
'Distant Early Warning' (5.15)
'Mystic Rhythms' (5.32)
'Witch Hunt' (4.00)

'The Rhythm Method' (4.37)
'The Rhythm Method' is not a new song – this is a drum solo. Peart's skilful use of dynamic control and the introduction of unexpected instrumentation (glockenspiel and sampled 'big-band' sounds) make this a masterclass in how to hit things with sticks. 'The Rhythm Method' was edited down to fit on the available running time of a CD at the time, the alterations being made with Peart's express approval. The final sound, a gong, segues us into...

'Force Ten' (4.55)
'Time Stand Still' (5.13)
'Red Sector A' (5.18)
'Closer To The Heart' (4.54)

Presto (1989)

Personnel:
Alex Lifeson: electric and acoustic guitars
Geddy Lee: vocals, bass, synthesisers
Neil Peart: drums and electronic percussion
Additional keyboards by Rupert Hine and Jason Sniderman
Additional background vocals by Rupert Hine
Recorded at Le Studio, Morin Heights and McClear Place, Toronto, between June and August 1989
Produced by Rupert Hine and Rush
Released: 21 November 1989
Label: Atlantic Records
Chart positions: Canada: 7, US: 13, UK: 10
All music composed by Lee and Lifeson, with lyrics by Peart

When the trio reconvened after a six-month break, they were ready to be a new, rockier version of themselves. A fresh contract was signed with Atlantic Records, as the band no longer felt that they were a priority for Mercury due to numerous personnel changes at the record company. The trio saw themselves as a 'cash-cow' which required little active promotion. In *Chemistry*, Neil reflected on the change of record label:

> We found ourselves free of deadlines and obligations for the first time in 15 years, so we decided to make the most of that. We took some time off, got to know ourselves and our families again, and generally just backed away from the infectious machinery of Rash – I mean Rush.

There was also a determination to return to a stripped-back sound, more in keeping with the changing musical landscape. Bands like Faith No More and Living Colour were fashionable with their fusion of funk and metal. Rush headed to Chalet Studio in the Toronto countryside to work on some new ideas, with the guitar back as the main focus of composition.

Peter Collins, feeling that he was partially responsible for the commercial underperformance of *Hold Your Fire*, bowed out. The hunt was on, yet again, for another producer. Rupert Hine, best known for his work with Stevie Nicks, Tina Turner, and 1980s pop star Howard Jones, was hired. Hine, the band's third English producer in a row, was tasked with moving Rush in a new direction. In an interview with *Metal Hammer* in March 2013, Geddy admitted that...

> ... I was getting sick of technology and wanted a return to a more basic approach. We were lucky in that our producer, Rupert Hine, agreed, so that's why it's more about the vocals than anything else. However, I have to say that the album didn't turn out the way we hoped. If there's one album we'd

love to do all over again, this is it. The songs are so much stronger than the way they came out.

Recording was completed in four months, mostly at Le Studio, with solos and vocals added at McClear Place. Mixing was carried out at Metropolis Studios in London in September 1989. *Presto* emerged two months later, with Geddy, in *Chemistry*, describing it as 'a kind of renewal to me. It's a renewal of energy and a positive outlook in musical terms and in personal terms, both in my place in the band and my feeling about recording.'

The cover is a monochromatic photograph of a magician's black top hat, with a rabbit inside, levitating above a grassy knoll. Eleven other bunnies populate the area, although at the start of the shoot, there'd only been a pair of them. On the rear of the sleeve are three pencil-drawn hands representing the game 'Rock, Paper, Scissors', an illustration inspired by the album's tenth track. The hands are Syme's own, drawn by him. Individual black and white portraits of the trio were taken by Andrew McNaughton; Lifeson is now the 'boy next door – rejected', Peart looks like he knows exactly where the bodies are buried and Lee is all sunglasses and ponytail.

The absence of colour in the cover reflects the sterile sound of the album's production. On the plus side, the synths have largely been put back in their cases, now serving a supportive role rather than dominating proceedings. What *Presto* lacks is enough good songs. 'The Pass', 'War Paint', 'Presto' and 'Available Light' are excellent, but much of the rest is merely adequate, occasionally pushing reasonable. Otherwise, there's little to really engage the listener's heart or mind.

'Show Don't Tell' (5.01)

The unexpected introduction style to 'Force Ten' on *Hold Your Fire* is maintained with *Presto*. 'Show Don't Tell' opens with some very quiet, hypnotic drums and a gradual crescendo of synth. The Rush of old then greet us with a loud, heavy, aggressive guitar-led riff, and what a joy it is to behold. The music calms for the verse as Lee gives voice to Peart's analysis of our impressions of people. His words portray a drama set in a court of law, and can be seen as a metaphor for the judgments we automatically make about others we encounter. The 'call-and-response' chorus is effective, and there is an intriguing funky feel running throughout, but the synths are still prominent, the instrumental section doesn't do much or go anywhere and Lifeson's contributions are again more textural than outstanding. The overall feel is one of clinical precision rather than passionate embrace.

'Chain Lightning' (4.33)

With a faster tempo and a more upbeat delivery, 'Chain Lightning' is a curious mix of driving, direct rock and lighter poppier moments, which ultimately doesn't work, leaving frustration in its wake. The verses have a straightforward groove, with the lyrics addressing the idea that joy and excitement are better when shared with someone else: 'when the moment dies, the spark still flies, reflected in another pair of eyes'. A catchy vocal melody and Lifeson's completely 'ad-hoc solo' (reversed in the studio, which is why it is so unplayable) are highlights, but again, the downsides dominate. The synthy chorus is light, fluffy and commercial, and there is the bizarre inclusion of the guitarist's spoken, pitch-altered 'That's nice' just before the end. Two tracks in, and the songwriting is nowhere near as strong as it should be.

'The Pass' (4.51)

A slower, thoughtful number, 'The Pass' gradually builds from its sparse beginnings into a brooding, powerful track that sensitively deals with a young person's suicide. The lyrics effectively compare a teenager's 'proud swagger out of the school yard, waiting for the world's applause' to a person now 'trembling on a rocky ledge, staring down into a heartless sea'. This is someone who 'can't face life on the razor's edge, nothing's what they thought it would be'. The contrast between the expectation of the young entering the adult world and the reality is superbly described here. In an interview with *Metal Hammer* in March 2013, Peart discussed his thoughts behind his lyrics:

> I spent a lot of time on it, refining it, and, even more, doing research ... So I really worked hard to find true stories ... what they felt, and why the people had taken this desperate step, and trying really hard fundamentally to understand something that to me is totally un-understandable. I wanted to de-mythologise it; take the nobility out of it. Let's not pretend it's a hero's end. It's not a triumph. It's a tragedy. It's a personal tragedy for them, but much more for the people left behind.

The central riff is played by Lee, with Lifeson adding sustained chord washes in the background as moody drumming contributes to the atmosphere. The vocal melody is memorable without being overtly commercial; Lee harmonises with himself with the excellent 'turn around, and turn around, and turn around' section. This culminates with the heartfelt 'don't turn your back and slam the door on me'. Lifeson's sustained, screaming solo builds into a repeat of the heavy chorus, which climaxes with Lee's highly effective, isolated 'Christ, what have you done?'

'The Pass' is magnificent – full of contrasts and intelligent perspectives – and it is a great shame that 'Presto' doesn't contain more songs of this calibre.

'War Paint' (5.24)

Some heavy rock energy dominates 'War Paint' with synths swirling behind some scything power chords. Another song dealing with the problems of youth, Peart examines how we enhance our appearances before facing the outside world of our peers and communities: the girl and boy checking their 'disguises'.

The music drives along with purpose and aggression, full of melody, with Lee yet again delivering the vocal goods, especially with the 'paint her name on a one way street ... paint the night with battle cries' section (0.53 – 1.08). This culminates with another of Peart's insightful couplets: 'All puffed up with vanity, we see what we want to see. To the beautiful and the wise, the mirror always lies'.

The heaviest section of the song is the final verse ('Boys and girls together, mistake conceit for pride...'), and the band sound fantastic here, powering away together with harmonised Lee vocals and some joyous chord work. There is an impressive solo (3.37 – 3.53) before 'War Paint' fades with repeated 'boys and girls together, let's paint the mirror black' because 'the mirror always lies'.

'Scars' (4.07)

Funky bass and some worryingly familiar keyboard moments show that Rush haven't entirely moved on from their synth era. 'Scars' sounds like it's an off-cut from the *Hold Your Fire* or *Power Windows* sessions. The instrumentation obscures the engaging lyrics, and the absence of many meaningful guitar contributions means that my attention begins to wander. The track sounds like a jam session that got out of hand. The relentless bass riff, the unaltering tempo and relative (for Peart) dull drum patterns all combine to make this mutated idea into a very ordinary composition, more reliant on plodding feel than musical creativity.

Peart's central idea – that emotional tragedies build upon each other, forming a type of shield around our soul and emotions – is an intriguing one. However, the refrain 'I get this feeling' soon begins to grate with its frequent repetition, and melodically, this song just isn't good enough to carry the words through with an appropriate connection due to its repetitive nature. The best part of the song is the chorus, where Lee's voice rises in pitch and conviction, but that's the high point.

'Scars' is a lyric that needs better music. What is presented to us may have worked better as an instrumental, or part of one, putting the words aside for better and more varied inspiration to come along. As it is, the relentless 4/4 funk groove soon begins to bore, with the song coming to a welcome finish with yet another repeat of the 'Scars of pleasure, scars of pain, atmospheric changes make them sensitive again' refrain.

'Presto' (5.46)

The title track has some suitably magical moments; the combination of the vocal melody and the strummed 12-string acoustic guitar is refreshing. The lyrics are equally excellent, dwelling as they do on expressions of genuine wonder. Another highlight is Lee's vocal performance throughout the song; he feels impassioned, none more so with his expression of the line 'I look down into a million houses, and wonder what you're doing tonight'.

Unfortunately, that which was tiresome on the last two albums returns for the chorus with breathy synths and a shiny feel, showing that the last vestiges of the 'synth era' have yet to be fully disposed of. Luckily, the acoustic guitar, excellent lyrics and top-notch singing return to restore the faith with the lines 'I had a dream of a winter's garden, a midnight rendezvous, silver, blue and frozen silence, what a fool I was for you' – the words blend effectively with the lush musical soundscape.

Things pick up considerably after the second chorus with the guitar dominating, and the much heavier section ('Don't ask me, I'm just improvising ...'), which moves into another spectacular, but too short, solo. The power increases for a reprise of this section, culminating with a dramatic 'I radiate more heat than light' with Lee almost returning to his 1970s vocal pitch. But then, it's another soft landing of a repeated chorus, which cruises past the ears a few more times, with overlaid vocals and guitar lines guiding the song to a comfortable rather than combative fade.

'Superconductor' (4.47)

'Superconductor', a companion piece to 'Limelight', would have made a far superior album opener; fast, taut, and lyrically biting, it drives along with conviction and commitment. The only thing missing from this otherwise excellent song is one of Lifeson's unhinged solos; here, the guitarist restricts himself to plenty of aggressive chord work.

Unusually for much of *Presto*, the opening riff strays off the well-beaten 4/4 path and revisits 7/4 time for the verses. The synths swamp the pre-chorus, but these are soon banished for the actual chorus, where Hine joins in on backing vocals.

Peart is scathing in his critique of popular fame: whether the 'star to be' is a male singer ('Packaged like a rebel or a hero, target mass appeal') or a female actor ('She's addicted to applause, the world a stage she never leaves it'), he is unrelenting in his highly critical attack on what he sees as the banality, and lack of integrity, he hears in modern 'manufactured' music.

The instrumental section (2.20 – 2.43) is an opportunity wasted; nothing much happens (perhaps that's the point ...), and the music is led by a simple, shiny synth melody.

The coda section has repeated choruses, rising in pitch from the original key of C major, through D major and E major, before returning to C major for an energetic push through to a final chord.

'Anagram (For Mongo)' (3.59)

Paraphrasing the line from Mel Brooks' 1974 film *Blazing Saddles* – 'Candygram for Mongo!' – Peart's choice of 'Anagram' is not a good one. The second half of each line is comprised of letters from the first half. On the page, this is merely wordplay: 'There's a snake coming out of the darkness/ Parade from paradise'. It goes on in this fashion through all its 36 lines. The lyrics reach 'Peak Clunk' with the abysmally clumsy couplet 'lonely things like nights I find end finer with a friend'.

It's back to 'Hold Your Power Windows' for the introduction, which is soon pushed out of the way by a pulsing electric guitar rhythm and the vocals. But the song is fundamentally routine; an average performance with a commercial-sounding chorus. The introduction reappears at the start of the instrumental (2.02 – 2.32), where the lead instrument is a piano, which is a pleasant change at least.

'Anagram (For Mongo)' is an exercise in pointless lyrical cleverness and second-rate musical ideas thrown together to produce something which satisfies in neither department. It ranks along 'red lenses' (*Grace Under Pressure*) as a further display of an uninspiring morass of pointless cleverness.

'Red Tide' (4.29)

This is a welcome return to lyrical integrity, with some powerful musical contributions. Piano and synth have a stranglehold on the introduction, but the first verse sees Peart back on point: 'Nature has a new plague to run in our streets, history some new wrinkle we are doomed to repeat'.

The tension builds with the pre-chorus before exploding with the dramatic 'This is not a false alarm, this is not a test'. The unrelenting dystopian vision presented on 'Red Tide' sounds like a return to *Grace Under Pressure*: 'Stay out of the sun, it only burns my skin, sky full of poison and the atmosphere's too thin'. But here, Peart is not one for giving in and accepting this fate: 'Now's the time to turn the tide, now's the time to fight', paraphrasing 'Do Not Go Gentle Into That Good Night', Dylan Thomas' famous 1951 poem ('Let us not go gently to the endless winter night').

Lifeson lets loose with a solo, which, again, is far too brief, the song ending with a short, sharp slap on the final quaver of the phrase. On the plus side, 'Red Tide' has plenty of power. On the minus side, the synths are doing too much for their own good. The piano again works as a change of texture, especially with the introductory ostinato, but for a song with much to say about a serious subject, the overall effect is less convincing due to the musical arrangement.

'Hand Over Fist' (4.11)

Initially composed as an instrumental, 'Hand Over Fist' features more funk, and this time it's Lifeson doing his best Nile Rodgers impression. The song opens with the chorus, which is lightweight and could have its eye on the pop charts. Luckily, a dirtier, funky guitar riff enters the fray for the verse, which is by far the best part of the composition. There's a suitably manic, soaring (and yet again too short) guitar solo before another excellent section (2.24 – 2.44) where the lyrics underline their point of open-mindedness winning the day: 'Take a walk outside myself in some exotic land, greet a passing stranger, feel the strength in his hand, feel my world expand'. Repeated choruses send this curio of a track into a fade with some additional guitar pyrotechnics in the background. 'Hand Over Fist' is yet another example of interesting lyrics being given only adequate musical support.

'Available Light' (5.02)
The title is a photographer's term for the degree of artificial lighting required for a shot. Peart takes this concept and superimposes it on his desire to experience life as it really is, with no fakery or tricks, not how it may be portrayed by others in a less-than-honest manner.

Fortunately, the album's final track is fantastic. Opening, uncharacteristically, with a sparse bluesy piano, bass and drum accompaniment, the regretful vocal is superb: 'The restless wind has seen all things in every kind of light ... in the canyons of the city you can hear the buildings cry'.

The tempo doubles, guitars and keyboards join the texture, exploding into the best music we've heard on *Presto* with anthemic vocals, powerful drums and excellent guitar contributions. The mood retreats to the bluesy opening with Lifeson adding tasty phrases in between the lyrics. 'Available Light' builds again into the chorus and an instrumental with another display of fretboard fabulousness, the song climaxing again with the magnificent reprise: 'All four winds together can't bring the world to me'.

The song powers its way to a fade, and this fan is left wishing that the rest of *Presto* was as uplifting and emotive as this. Lee excels vocally, Lifeson and Peart are on top form and the disparate elements merge to produce something bigger and better than its parts.

Overall, *Presto* is a listenable, competent piece of work, with some indications of a return to *Moving Pictures* levels of quality, but at the same time, it can be a frustrating record, where too much of what is heard doesn't really need to be listened to again. This frustration was borne out by comments in *Contents Under Pressure* from Geddy when offering up his opinions of the release, having completed the follow-up, *Roll The Bones*:

> I think the songwriting on *Presto* is inferior to *Roll The Bones*. I think we experimented with some things on *Presto* that came to fruition on *Roll The Bones*. In a way, *Presto* is a warm-up to *Roll The Bones*. I think there are some very, very strong songs on *Roll The Bones*, and I can't say that of *Presto*. I don't think it's our strongest album from a songwriting point of view.

Roll The Bones (1991)

Personnel:
Alex Lifeson: electric and acoustic guitars, backing vocals
Geddy Lee: vocals, bass, synthesisers
Neil Peart: drums and cymbals
Additional keyboards and background vocals by Rupert Hine
Recorded at Le Studio, Morin Heights and McClear Place, Toronto, between February and May 1991
Produced by Rupert Hine and Rush
Engineered by Stephen W. Taylor
Released: 3 September 1991
Label: Atlantic Records
Chart positions: Canada: 11, US: 3, UK: 10
All music composed by Lee and Lifeson, lyrics by Peart, except 'Where's My Thing?', music by Lee and Lifeson

Night follows day, tour follows album and the good Rush ship set sail again in February 1990 on a 70-date extravaganza. The *Presto* tour concluded with a renewed enthusiasm to return to the studio. *Presto* had avoided an overarching theme. When it came to the band's 14th album, Peart, as ever armed with notebooks filled with phrases and ideas, came across a scribble from years ago, 'Roll the Bones', an expression for the throwing of dice. Peart had come upon the title via a sci-fi story he had read in the 1970s by Fritz Leiber called 'Gonna Roll The Bones'. Chance and its potential for good or ill seemed a good starting point.

Ideas for songs were thrown around in Toronto at the end of 1990, with the band moving to Chalet Studios in Claremont, north of Toronto, for writing and arranging. In early 1991, the trio reunited with producer Rupert Hine and ventured back into Le Studio to record. This was followed by time in McClear Place, Toronto, for vocal overdubs, with mixing completed at Nomis Studios in London.

The cover is linked with the album's theme of fate. A young boy wearing a black tee-shirt, jeans and trainers walks along a well-trodden, narrow, concrete path, idly kicking a skull in front of him (another bone, rolling). To his right is a wall constructed entirely of dice. To his left is a dark waterway, which looks oily and threatening. Lost in a world of his own, the child is unconcerned with any potential danger. The juxtaposition of the boy's innocence with the 'wall of chance' and the potential for injury or death nearby is striking.

Artist Hugh Syme, another long-time feature of the Rush machine, won the 1992 Juno award for his work on *Roll The Bones* in the category of 'Best Album Cover Design'.

On the other side of the cover is a close-up of the dice wall with a rectangle missing. Three femur bones are floating through the gap, through which a blue and slightly cloudy sky is seen. Inside, the allusions to fate continue with a striking image of three wishbones floating above a calm sea at sunset. They appear to be 'walking the face of the earth'. Individual earth-toned images of the band show Lifeson (serious face, hands in smart-casual dark jacket), Peart (short of hair, black of roll-neck) and Lee (semi-mimicking Lifeson but with the addition of see-through shades). It's all very sombre and subdued.

Roll The Bones is a real mixed bag. It is more sonically engaging than its predecessor, with plenty of energy and a freshness to the recorded sound, building on the progress of *Presto*. But, again, some of the songs fail to impress or leave much of a mark on the memory. 'Dreamline', 'Face Up', 'The Big Wheel' and 'You Bet Your Life' all work well, and the inclusion of an instrumental ('Where's My Thing?') is a good showcase of the band embracing funk into their ever-widening stylistic repertoire.

Elsewhere, the synth-pop legacy, whilst diminished, lives on, and the inclusion of some rap is either innovative and refreshing, or clunky and awkward, depending upon your point of view. The songs that fail to connect do so more because of the music than the lyrics; Peart remains, by and large, sharp and relevant. And like the two albums of the Collins era, there are just enough decent songs on *Presto* and *Roll The Bones* combined to make one really good album.

'Dreamline' (4.38)

After the quiet sound effect of a lorry driving left to right in the stereo mix, 'Dreamline' establishes itself as a pacy, exciting song packed with melody, drive and energy. The repeating guitar arpeggio has a confident edge, and in keeping with the album's theme, this is a song that merges everyday life with an individual's dreams. Life is presented as both a matter of luck and the taking of chances – win, lose or draw.

The song gets through its introduction, first verse and chorus in under a minute. Similarly, Peart's economy of words conveys much with little. A punchy, descending three-note brass synth motif (lifted from 'Distant Early Warning') is extremely effective in changing the mood from the reflective to the powerful, and kudos must go to Lee's voice, which, once again, shines across the album.

The chorus is the highlight of the song, and indeed the album; full of spirit and yet combining a carefully crafted melody with some impressive words – 'Learning that we're only immortal, for a limited time' – here, the virtual absence of guitar serves to underline the power of the lyrics; its absence focussing the ears more on the import of the words, which capture the fleeting moments of youth when anything seems possible, before life gets in the way.

Lifeson shines with one of his typically idiosyncratic, freewheeling solos (3.00 – 3.26), and repeated choruses bring this fine first track to a tight end.

'Bravado' (4.35)
In complete contrast, 'Bravado' is relentlessly under-tempo and sounds laboured. As a consequence, the largely unaltering dynamics, texture and the repeated refrain wear the ears down. This is a shame as the lyrics rework the Greek legend of Icarus, who escaped imprisonment with his inventor father Daedalus, using wings made from feathers and wax. Ignoring his father's warnings, Icarus flew too close to the sun, causing his wings to melt and him to fall to an unnecessary death. Peart posits that it is better to reach for your desires, even when failure is the more likely option. There is a form of victory in giving your best to the endeavour, even if you are unsuccessful.

Unfortunately, musically, 'Bravado' trudges. Guitars chime, keyboards sustain and the vocals sound suitably regretful. The music sounds mundane and uninspired; not suitable material for what Lee is singing about. The inclusion of an isolated acoustic guitar or a piano could have worked wonders here. As it is, the relatively unchanging accompaniment doesn't serve the words well. Lifeson's solo (his 'demo' version was transplanted into the finished track) is suitably mournful and restrained, not over-played, just conveying emotion without becoming overwrought. Peart's drumming is continually inventive and occasionally surprising within the consistency of the 4/4 time signature. In an interview with 'Guitar Player' in November 1991, Lifeson expanded on the inclusion of his 'placeholder' solo:

> When we're developing the arrangement in the writing stages, I toss a solo on tape so we have something to listen to. It's late at night, the lights are down low and I'm by myself. These were supposed to be throwaway solos, but when it was time to do the 'real' solos, Neil had already adjusted his parts to fit what I had played. So it came down to me trying to recreate everything, which doesn't work. You might improve the sound, but even if you play exactly the same notes, you'll never capture that magic feel. The solos in 'Ghost Of A Chance' and 'Bravado' are certainly my favourites on the record, if not among my favourite solos ever. When I listen to them, I hear the way I felt at that time. That's really the key.

The outro of the song features multiple layers of Lee repeatedly singing the refrain: 'We will pay the price, but we will not count the cost'. Whilst by this stage, the song has become heavier, with greater emphasis on the guitar sound and busier drumming, it really doesn't build into anything as special as the words require.

'Bravado' is an irritation, a strong lyric linked to average, plodding music that outstays its welcome. The song's inclusion in subsequent live albums always feels like a wasted opportunity to expose other, better material. Sounding more like a requiem than a defiant call to arms, 'Bravado' should have been ... braver.

'Roll The Bones' (5.30)

Rush meets rap. And funk. And synth pop. Oh, and there's some rock thrown in as well. A fine example of the 'pot-pourri' approach of the album, the title track doesn't stand head and shoulders above the other songs despite the drive and invention in the pre-chorus section. Again, the 'Why are we here? Because we're here' chorus refrain starts to irritate due to frequent repetition. Lyrically, Peart again offers much within a few well-worded phrases. The pre-chorus ('We go out in the world and take our chances, fate is just the weight of circumstances, that's the way that Lady Luck dances, roll the bones') neatly sums up the theme: never being able to foretell the future should never prevent us from taking chances. It is better to try and fail than to fail to try, as Peart might have written.

The infamous/innovative (delete as appropriate) 'rap' section is intriguing or downright bizarre. The rap (3.12 – 3.42, and again at 3.51 – 4.14), coming after the soaring, evocative, but far too brief guitar solo, has a detuned Geddy sounding most un-Lee-like. According to producer Hine, John Cleese, the English comedian and writer, was in the frame for the recording. Also considered was Robbie Robertson, of The Band fame. Hine himself attempted the section, and then suggested that Lee give it a go.

The song's final minute has the repeating refrain, and it goes on for too long. The point has been made, and reminding us only serves to reinforce the idea that some greater variation or creativity was needed for the fade.

'Face Up' (3.54)

Putting the dice down and picking up the playing cards as a new metaphor, 'Face Up' continues the theme of luck and how we react to its arrival. The song starts well with plenty of energetic guitars, putting aside the irritating high-pitched keyboard additions. The athletic drumming is the central driving force of this track, again showing how creative Peart can be within the relative restrictions of 4/4 time.

Lyrically, we are encouraged to face whatever life throws at us, whichever hand we are dealt. The chorus has a catchy refrain with a sing-along quality, and there is a sudden change of mood to a half-time tempo at 1.54 with some sustained, atmospheric synths, which act as a suitably reflective backdrop for the bridge section. This is brutally interrupted by a spectacular, but again too short, guitar solo. Repeated choruses drive this excellent, committed rocker to an almost powerful end. Some sustained synth is allowed to drift past the final chord, making the outro less convincing.

'Where's My Thing?' (3.49)

Amusingly subtitled as 'Part IV of the Gangster of Boats Trilogy' (an album title 'threatened' by Lee and Lifeson to persuade Peart to come up with something 'better'), 'Where's My Thing?' is the band's first instrumental since 'YYZ', a decade ago. Based around some fast funk rhythms and more impressive drumming, it lacks the hard rock power, dexterous demonstrations of phenomenal technique and melodic and stylistic invention that made 'YYZ' so special. It is, however, still a reasonably entertaining listen with some interesting moments.

There are two main themes: a funky melodic guitar riff and a sustained keyboard melody of some symphonic grandeur. These form a verse/chorus template for much of the piece. This is broken only by a wonderfully dirty guitar riff at 1.50, where the band's 'prog-chops' are briefly brought out of the attic over three bars of 4/4 and a single bar of 5/4, followed by two further bars of 4/4.

At 2.15, there is a beautiful, anguished and sustained solo that sounds too distant due to the amount of reverb added in the studio. This leads into a reprise of the main themes, and a welcome return of Lifeson's riff at 3.29, where the band resolutely groove away for a traditional eight bars of 4/4 time. A strong ending is spoiled by a splashy off-beat synth chord. A super-tight finish would have been cleaner and therefore more effective.

'The Big Wheel' (5.12)

Once we're past the *Hold Your Fire*-isms of the introduction (lots of swirly synths dominate an otherwise fierce opening), a great, swinging guitar rhythm establishes a song with some proper feel and attitude to it. 'The Big Wheel' is a bold rocker with a commercial edge, especially with its catchy chorus, and once again, Lee sings with conviction.

The verses are punchy and persuasive, and whilst the chorus features the dubious (for Rush) line 'looking for love', this is another song with the theme of chance running through it. This slight lyrical 'dink' – including the rhyming of 'chance' and romance' in the fourth verse – doesn't dent the enjoyment of this otherwise excellent marriage of words, melody and performance.

The introduction is repeated after the second chorus with an extended bridge section, where many overlaid Lees prefigure the production stylings of *Vapor Trails* (Lee would record many takes of him singing the background vocals to create a 'Choir Of Geddys'). Here, the words move away from an autobiographical stance to a more generalist observation on the nature of fate: 'Wheel goes round, landing on a leap of fate. Life redirected in ways unexpected, sometimes the odd number wins. The way the big wheel spins'. Repeated choruses take this well-above-average song into a fade.

'Heresy' (5.25)

'Heresy' has the feel of a big pop-stadium ballad, carefully crafted for commercial consumption. Musically, it sounds like 1980s Rush-by-numbers going through the motions, with plenty of readily identifiable features failing to create a song which matches the flair and attack of its words. Pointed but ultimately pointless, 'Heresy' joins 'Bravado' in the 'Underachiever' category with ease. This is a pity as Lee and Lifeson fail to give Peart's angry, accurate and damning critique of the legacy of Communism the appropriate musical justice.

The track is comfortably mid-tempo in 4/4 and lacks a vocal melody to match the passion of the words. The vocals are sung without much conviction or bite (and therefore perfectly match the accompaniment) along with the sub-optimal section at 2.04, which contains the lame lyric, 'Do we have to be forgiving at last? What else can we do? Do we have to say goodbye to the past? Yes, I guess we do'.

Despite Peart's angular, African-themed drum patterns, the majority of the rest of the sound is filled with inappropriate synth and chiming guitars. Where's the distortion, the passion, the desire to match words to music? Ultimately, 'Heresy' is an opportunity missed; what could have been a rousing, blistering heavy rock number really just flows past the ears, the soporific accompaniment smothering some fine thoughts.

'Ghost Of A Chance' (5.18)

Another chunk of routine Rush pop-rock, 'Ghost Of A Chance' chugs along without incident; a steady tempo, in 4/4 time yet again, a straightforward central riff and a relaxed and uneventful vocal melody all contribute to the temptation to hit the 'skip' button.

However, at 1.04, the mood utterly alters as the track adopts a soft, bluesy setting. Here, the sustained synths and Lifeson's tasteful noodling add much to the vocals. Peart's long-held and well-broadcast lack of belief in 'the stars or the planets' or 'an angel watching from afar' is contrasted with his view that 'there's a ghost of a chance we can find someone to love, and make it last'. Lifeson adds a gorgeous, simple, sustained melody to the tail of this section.

Then, it's 'as you were' with the return of the opening instrumentation and feel. Despite the relative banality of the music, the lyrics still hit home: 'Like a million little crossroads through the backstreets of youth, each time we turn a corner, a tiny moment of truth'. Here, Peart underlines the nature of chance and possibility at any given time or place in one's life, neatly extending the aphorism 'You never know what's round the corner'.

Suddenly, we're back into the jazz nightclub texture, which is extended with a lyrical guitar solo over a stronger bass and drum rhythm. The track then falls back into the relaxed mood with some stylish piano joining the guitar interjections, fading away with more of Lifeson's fine melodic lines.

'Neurotica' (4.40)

The is another example of both Peart's wordplay set to music, and the band's continuing inability to completely shed the electronic sound from their songs. 'Neurotica' could have been lifted from any of the three preceding albums.

The chorus (rhyming 'neurotica' with 'exotica', 'erotica', 'hypnotica', 'psychotica', and 'chaotica') is notable more for the overlaid vocals than anything else. The following verse is incredibly clunky: 'You just don't get it, baby, don't you ask yourself why? If you don't like the answer, forget it, you know I hate to see you cry'.

The outstanding part of this otherwise mundane composition is Lifeson's excellent, frenetic solo (3.25 – 3.41). This is full of the passion and power absent elsewhere. Impressive playing by all three musicians doesn't disguise the fact that 'Neurotica' delivers little beyond a wish to quickly move onto the final song.

'You Bet Your Life' (4.59)

Things pick up for the finale, 'You Bet Your Life', which is bright, bouncy and almost poppy in sound, and the chorus sounds like the trio are committed to making this a suitable ending. Here, the multi-layered vocals ('The odds get even') are highly effective and suitably powerful, sung over some strongly syncopated chords; this section would even make a good crowd sing-along section in concert

Lyrically, this is a restatement of the album's central themes. This is reality, and you have to deal with it, take your chances and make the best of things. There is also another opportunity for some more rap (oh good), but this raises eyebrows to a lesser degree as it is performed against a driving rock rhythm. This highly wordy section (1.40 – 2.08 and 3.20 – 4.18) sees Peart maybe having a dig at the many critics who have attempted to put the trio in 'this' or 'that' box. This is implied throughout the rant, which explicitly mocks the many and varied labels applied to a person or group of whom one is critical.

The song goes into a fade just as Lifeson is getting his teeth and fingers into another emotion-filled solo. This is another of the album's shortcomings; when the guitarist is on fire, allow him to burn; don't snuff him out like a candle with a fader.

Counterparts (1993)

Personnel:
Alex Lifeson: electric and acoustic guitars
Geddy Lee: vocals, bass, synthesisers
Neil Peart: drums, cymbals, electronic percussion
Additional keyboards by John Webster
Orchestration on 'Nobody's Hero' arranged and conducted by Michael Kaman
Recorded at Le Studio, Morin Heights and McClear Pathe, Toronto, between April and June 1993
Produced by Peter Collins and Rush
Released: 19 October 1993
Label: Atlantic Records
Chart positions: Canada: 6, US: 2, UK: 14
All music composed by Lee and Lifeson, with lyrics by Peart, except 'Between The Sun And Moon', lyrics by Peart and Dubois

By the early 1990s, the musical landscape had shifted again, and Rush, ever a mirror for prevailing trends, responded in kind. Bands including Soundgarden, Pearl Jam and Nirvana were now leading the way with an exciting, stripped-back sound. Rush wanted to follow in their wake. Despite the critical approval of their recent output, the band were hankering to return to a more basic style. They were aware that the power of their live shows was at odds with the relative sterility and perfectionist sound of their recent studio releases. In *Beyond The Lighted Stage*, Alex said:

> *Counterparts* turned out to be the record that we envisioned when we first started working on it. The songs were thicker and (had) more hair on them.

Geddy agreed:

> That record is a big turning point in reconnecting with the kind of rock 'n' roll guts of Rush.

Writing and rehearsals began in March 1993, with Lee and Lifeson riffing away to a drum machine, whilst the lyricist turned his attention to the evergreen and universal subject of relationships, with duality becoming a running theme. The album title came to Peart as he was reviewing the various sets of lyrics. Realising that his words covered all people of all sexualities, 'counterpart' seemed appropriate. In *Chemistry*, Neil remembered:

> I was thinking certainly about gender difference, and I've been reading Jung, so I was interested in the anima, the female spirit within the male, etc. I've been thinking a lot about the nature of heroism and what was good and bad about it, and the idea of a role model, and people I'd known

> in my own life who were important to me as influences but weren't important to the rest of the world. Duality became the only unifying theme. I ransacked everything from *Scientific American* to what great thinkers of the world have had to say about it ... I started free-associating through the lyrics and I pulled the word 'counterpoint' out of the song 'Animate'. When I looked it up in the dictionary and saw how complex its meaning was, that it meant both an opposite and a duplicate, I thought A-ha! That's what I'm writing about here, that's racism, culturalism, men and women, gays and straights, all of us, we're counterparts because we're the same but different.

The band needed a new producer. Somewhat surprisingly, Peter Collins returned to the fold. This was another first for Rush – re-employing a previous producer. For his part, Collins had been instrumental in the success of *After The War* for Gary Moore, *Operation: Mindcrime* and *Empire* for Queensrÿche, and *The Art Of Rebellion* by Suicidal Tendencies.

Kevin 'Caveman' Shirley was recruited as the recording engineer. Shirley had a very different method for capturing the band's sound, adopting a 'feel over detail' approach. Spontaneity was the key, with the intention of achieving the most natural 'as it happened' performance as possible. The recording sessions progressed swiftly with Collins at the helm. A fresh pair of ears, attached to Australian engineer Michael Letho, supervised the mixing process and added some refinement to the raw tracks.

The artwork played on the title effectively. It was as stripped back to its bare basics as the sound contained within. Engraved on the clear plastic cover of the CD is a gold-coloured nut and bolt, one just entering the other. The actual cover booklet is a deep blue with a central black rectangle over which the nut and bolt appear. This outwardly simplistic design is swept away by the massively detailed inner fold-out lyric sheet, which contains numerous images of differing interpretations of the album title.

The recorded sound is mighty. It's as if, sonically, the last decade never happened. Whilst keyboards are heard, their role is relegated to strictly one of occasional support. The guitars are huge, the bass playing and vocals sound excellent and the drums are alive with energy and attack. The first six songs are all top quality, but then things begin to veer off course. *Counterparts* is, for the most part, the sound of a reinvigorated group playing their hearts out and sounding as good, if not better, than they did in 1981.

'Animate' (5.05)

In *Contents Under Pressure*, Geddy said:

> I love 'Animate'. I think it's one of the great songs we've done. There's something about the bestiality of that song, the insistence of it.

Good point, well made. As if to emphasise the 'live' sound that we are going to experience, 'Animate' opens with the sound of Peart counting in the track. This is another first, and an indication of intent; this album is going to rock! The introduction, consisting of thunderous drums, pulsating bass, droning guitar and, in the background, an organ, all kick in. The band sound fantastic, focused and back to what they do best – playing intelligent, melodic, powerful rock music.

The song alternates between the chorus ('Polarise me ... elevate me') and a wondrous verse supported by a terrifically heavy, funky rock guitar riff ('Goddess in my garden ... ancient queen of inner space'). At 3.19, an eight-bar instrumental interrupts proceedings. This mixes a distant, sustained, distorted guitar solo with bubbling bass and African drum rhythms over which the bridge section vocals appear. Lifeson plays a wonderful bluesy-based solo before the continuation of this reflective section. An orchestral string effect is added to the chord progression as the track goes into a fade.

'Stick It Out' (4.31)

Opening with a monumentally heavy riff which hangs on the edge of feedback, 'Stick It Out 'is all swagger and testosterone, a mood we have rarely heard from Rush. Aggressive, pacy and possessing an almost manic, barely contained energy, the song is one of the heaviest tracks the band have ever recorded, even if the opening verse ('Trust to your instinct if it's safely restrained, lightning reactions must be carefully trained') is poor, as it fails to match the confidence and attack of the accompanying music.

The chorus is first class, with multiple Lees sounding superb amidst all the power and passion. The bridge section at 2.09 calms the mood down, and again, the words seem clumsy within the setting – 'Each time we bathe our reactions in artificial light' – only coming back on stream with the final couplet: 'You get so used to surrender, running back to cover your neck'.

Lifeson unleashes another one of his completely over-the-top solos, a superb demonstration of what a distorted electric guitar is capable of. Despite the obvious phallic references, Peart is asking the listener to admit to their individual faults and failings, to accept and deal with them in order to live a better life as a more honest person. The fact that this theme is delivered with such a sonic bombardment is a testament to the band's skills at transposing intelligent ideas into inspiring and uplifting music.

'Cut To The Chase' (4.49)

The goodies keep coming. Initially relatively calm and controlled with some simple electric guitar arpeggios, pulsing bass and, erm, a tambourine, the song grows in power, exploding into a riff of monolithic magnificence that underpins the chorus, the lyrics of which detail the importance of the quest and drive for creativity: 'You may be right, it's all a waste of time, I guess that's just a chance I'm prepared to take, a danger I'm prepared to face, cut to the chase'.

The second verse has a busier texture behind the fine vocals with a crescendo into the chorus, again full of attack and spirit. Lifeson then throws in another off-the-wall, extraordinarily freewheeling solo. Rising to 'Something For Nothing' (*2112*) levels of conviction and persuasion, the song builds still further with Lee proclaiming 'I'm old enough not to care too much about what you think of me' and 'But I'm young enough to remember the future and the way things ought to be'. Poignant, powerful, and persuasive, this is yet another example of when Rush get it right, they *really* get it right.

The chorus returns, cruising in top gear with the incongruous decoration of some delicate piano lines before the track comes to an abrupt halt. This 'new/old' Rush is making some great rock music again.

'Nobody's Hero' (4.56)
A briskly strummed acoustic guitar recalls 'Making Memories' (*Fly By Night*). 'Nobody's Hero', however, strikes a sombre, realistic note with its tale of two unnamed individuals, one a homosexual male who has died of AIDS (this was a reference to a gay friend of Peart's when he lived in London), the other a girl who has suffered an unspecified 'nightmare of brutality'. This was another true-life example; Kirsten French was a victim of serial rapist and murderer Paul Bernardo in Ontario. Both left grieving friends and family behind.

Highly melodic throughout, Lee's vocals and Kamen's gently swelling orchestration lead into the dramatic chorus. Here, Peart bemoans the fact that this person's death does not receive the same level of attention as someone the media has chosen to frame as a hero; the saver of a drowning child, the curer of a 'wasting disease', someone who lands a 'crippled airplane' or solves 'great mysteries'. Peart sees a disparity between the value of a human life as lived by a non-celebrity compared to that of a person who is famous for one reason or another.

This stance feeds into Lifeson's emotive, restrained solo, and the subsequent choruses are buoyed by an eloquent string section. 'Nobody's Hero' is a superb, thoughtful song which moves from quiet beginnings to an almost cinematic fade by its conclusion with ease and skill.

'Between The Sun And Moon' (4.38)
Lifeson sets up another excellent, syncopated, overdriven groove, which is kicked up several gears by the addition of bass and drums as Lee gives voice to the sometimes opaque lyrics: 'There is a space between sun and moon, not too many know about, in the silence between whisper and shout, the space between wonder and doubt'.

The chorus, obviously Dubois' work ('Ah, yes to yes to ah, ah to yes, why the sun, why the sun?'), is a thing of greatness – melodic, rousingly anthemic and catchy. It's a case of 'never mind the words, feel the music'. It doesn't really matter what the words actually are or what they mean at this point; the sense of elation and positivity in the music makes such analysis pointless.

In *Chemistry* Neil discussed working on lyrics that Pye Dubois had already submitted:

> I'm always concerned with Pye, 'Do you think I'm wrecking your work?' because theoretically, when he finishes it, he thinks it's done. But he seems comfortable with it, too.

At 2.39, the band reach back into their influences, suddenly sounding like The Who at one of their heavy peaks; the power chords rain down and Peart drums up a storm. Following this, Lifeson's solo verges on modern country fingerboard stylings, with a couple of his idiosyncratic, improvisatory touches.

'Between The Sun And Moon' is another fascinating facet of the rejuvenated Rush; a song with plenty of light and shade, dynamic contrasts and energetic performances makes this another fine addition to the collection.

'Alien Shoe' (5.48)

Alien Shore begins with the sound of Lifeson speak-singing, through pinched nostrils, 'Out of my nose'. Once that's out of the way, as it were, an introductory riot of howling guitar, energetic bass and agitated sounding drums soon gains some kind of equilibrium. The verses use the ocean as a metaphor for a relationship, with depths to explore 'in a struggle to be happy and free, swimming in a primitive sea'.

The chorus is another blinder, built around a repeated heavy rising guitar riff, the only downside being the words: 'For you and me sex is not a competition, for you and me sex is not a job description, for you and me – we agree'. Seriously? A 'job description'? At least it rhymes. The song relaxes back into its second verse with Peart making the point that, irrespective of 'colour and culture, language and race', we are all 'just variations on a theme, islands in a much larger stream'. We are all counterparts in some way, shape or form to each other. Lifeson's solo embodies elements of jazz and blues in the midst of all the distortion, delay and reverb.

The song comes further unstuck lyrically in the extended final chorus ('For you and me, we hold these truths to be self-evident. For you and me we'd elect each other president'). Given Peart's unmatched skill as a lyricist, this couplet is a rare low point, in my opinion.

'The Speed Of Love' (5.02)

Consistently mid-paced and sounding like another *Presto* leftover, 'The Speed Of Love' highlights a reappearance of the influence of The Police. Some 'over-production' values, in the form of plenty of effects-laden keyboards, maintain the sense that this song was discarded from previous efforts. Consequently, it's the first song on *Counterparts* to disappoint. Despite a tuneful chorus and refrain, the endeavour feels laboured, underpowered and lacking in conviction. There is an overwhelming sense of motions being gone through, and this is reflected in Lifeson's routine, languid, spacious solo.

The words promise more; the first verse ('Love is born with lightning bolts, electro-magnetic force. Burning skin and fireworks, a storm on a raging course') deserves greater musical energy than it receives. The song also goes on for too long; the last minute could have been excised without damaging the track's limited appeal.

Whilst all three players contribute with their usual level of technical proficiency and creativity, ironically, it doesn't sound like their hearts are really in this one.

'Double Agent' (4.52)

This is a real oddity. One of the last songs to be written for the album, here we are in the twilight world of indecision and opportunities, where everything is shades of grey. The song, unexpectedly, also extols the benefits of a good night's sleep, letting the subconscious make the decision for you.

The most 'proggy', or outright weird track on this or many previous albums, 'Double Agent' is a pot boiler of several conflicting musical ideas, all glued together by a resolute tempo. There are three themes: the chorus ('Where would you rather be? Anywhere, anywhere but here ...') is standard Rush for the period – tuneful, steady and in 4/4. The second section features an incredibly dense and intense guitar riff in 3/4 with Lee speaking the verse words (with the occasional sung interjection). The third section ('Wilderness of mirrors ...'), also in 3/4 time, has him returning to singing with a solid rhythmic backing:

0.00: First chorus
0.32: First spoken word verse
1.10: 'Wilderness of Mirrors ...'
1.33: Second chorus
2.05: Second spoken word verse
2.30: 'Wilderness of Mirrors ...'
2.54: Third chorus
3.26: Guitar solo over a pulverising 3/4 pulse
3.57: 'Wilderness of Mirrors ...'
4.20: Fourth spoken word verse, leading to a tight end

Whether it's the close-recorded voice in the verses, Lifeson's unconventional solo (where he plays a rapidly trilled low single note for four bars before repeating the idea an octave higher seconds later) or the effective lyrics ('Wilderness of mirrors, streets of cold desire, my precious sense of honour just a shield of rusty wire, I hold against the chaos and the cross of holy fire'), there is much to enjoy here.

'Leave That Thing Alone' (4.06)
The same cannot be said for this instrumental. Built around a lame funk guitar rhythm and supported by sequenced synthesiser, 'Leave That Thing Alone' is clearly cut from the same cloth as its predecessor on *Roll The Bones*. There is an expansive and reasonably engaging guitar refrain, Peart incorporates some African drum patterns in places and Lee's bass is consistently busy, but 'Leave That Thing Alone' sounds like a jam session in need of some better melodic ideas and tighter structuring.

The ears prick up at 1.12 with an impressive rising guitar riff in 6/4 time, which then develops into a jazz-rock style interlude. Lifeson's solo is instantly identifiable, but it is not amongst his best work, despite the guitarist stretching the upper reaches of his guitar neck to near breaking point.

In the end, which could have come sooner, this is a strange mix of differing, disjointed styles. The music fades away, highlighting further the aimlessness of the track. The title is unintentionally accurate. This is a thing that should have been left alone. Sadly, it wasn't.

'Cold Fire' (4.27)
Luckily, 'Cold Fire' restores the quality quota with an up-tempo aggressive burst of chord riffing to which purposeful bass and drums are added. The mood opens up almost immediately with a quieter, highly atmospheric verse, where the dual melodies of voice and beautifully phrased clean arpeggios create a magical feel. The degree of reverb adds much to this section, which builds with the refrain 'I'll be around, if you don't let me down too far, I'll be around, if you don't let me down'.

The second verse explores this observation of a male/female relationship, where the woman is the more realistic and forceful of the two. This is underlined spectacularly with the explosive 'This is not a love song, this isn't fantasy land' at 1.37. Peart's skills as a wordsmith are on no better display than with his metaphors for the 'cold fire' of love in a relationship: 'the phosphorescent wave on a tropical sea' and 'the pattern of moonlight on the bedroom floor'.

Lifeson's solo at 2.34 has his fingers flying all over the fretboard with a thin, distorted tone before the opening riff and the chorus reassert their power. Repeats of the refrain, the main riff and some spectacular drum fills take this excellent rocker into a fade.

'Everyday Glory' (5.11)
Sadly, this momentum is not maintained with the final track, which is an appropriately mid-tempo and melodically uninspiring trudge through 'Everyday people' with their 'everyday shame, everyday promises, shot down in flames'. Another song that drags hints of Hine into its mix, it's a shame that the music disappoints, as the lyrics draw their pictures well.

The first verse focuses on a mother and father in the middle of a furious row whilst their only child hides away, 'shaking with her hands over her ears, pushing back the tears till the pain disappears'. The second verse broadens this horizon to include 'the city where nobody smiles and nobody dreams; the city where desperation drives the bored to extremes'. These two verses focus on the intensely personal suffering – a place where there is little, if any happiness, and trouble is only a moment away.

Despite these powerful lyrics, 'Everyday Glory' comes over as another merely adequate Rush song, an underachiever compared to the majority of this album. It does at least end on an optimistic note with Peart hoping that 'if the future's looking dark', we're the ones who will 'have to shine', 'draw the line', 'have to try' and 'have to fly'. Here, his oft-repeated theme of self-reliance and individuals making the future better for themselves and hopefully others makes another appearance as the album's closing message.

Summarising *Counterparts* in *Contents Under Pressure*, Geddy said:

> *Counterparts* was definitely a reaction against that whole keyboard thing, there's no question in my mind. We had pushed that to the limit. I would say that through the end of working with Rupert and having now done two or three tours in this kind of slavish live mode, I think I was starting to have some frustration. And I think the writing of *Counterparts* reflected that. That's why there are very few keyboards on that record, kind of token keyboards. And really, they're not even necessary when I hear them, the little bits of keyboard parts that are still there. It's kind of a habit that was dying hard.

Test For Echo (1996)

Personnel:
Alex Lifeson: electric and acoustic guitars
Geddy Lee: vocals, bass, synthesisers
Neil Peart: drums, cymbals, hammered dulcimer
Recorded at Bearsville Studios, Catskills Mountains, New York State, and Reaction Studios, Toronto, between January and April 1996
Mixed at McClear Pathe
Produced by Peter Collins and Rush
Released: 10 September 1996
Label: Atlantic Records
Chart positions: Canada: 3, US: 5, UK: 25
All music composed by Lee and Lifeson, with lyrics by Peart, except 'Test For Echo' lyrics by Peart and Dubois, and 'Limbo', music by Lee, Lifeson and Peart

A two-month, 54-show *Counterparts* tour began in January 1994, taking in dates in the United States, with only two gigs in Canada.

Three years had elapsed between *Counterparts* and the band's 16th studio album. Despite commercial and critical success, exhaustion with the relentless write/record/release/tour cycle was bearing down on the trio. Lifeson felt that *Counterparts*, whilst being a good step in the right direction, hadn't gone far enough. For his part, Lee had recently become a father again and wanted to be much more involved in family life than he had been able to in the past. Peart, as always, had no shortage of hobbies and interests with which to indulge himself. A break from each other, and the Rush behemoth, was both a welcome and a necessary diversion.

The extended 'lay-off' afforded each player the opportunity to explore life outside the band. Lifeson released a solo album, *Victor*, a dark and intense affair, in January 1996. Peart, believing his drumming had reached 'peak Peart', felt the need for greater inspiration and instruction to become a better player. He took lessons with the legendary jazz drummer and teacher Freddie Gruber. As well as refining his technique, teacher and pupil became firm friends. Meanwhile, Lee devoted his time to his family.

Fans concerned with such a lengthy hiatus had their hunger for more Rush partially sated when a number of high-profile rock musicians (including Mike Portnoy, Billy Sheehan, Jake E Lee, Sebastian Bach, Steve Morse, Stuart Hamm, John Petrucci, George Lynch and Eric Martin, amongst others) recorded an album of Rush songs. *Working Man – A Tribute To Rush* was released in August 1996 on Magna Carta Records. Consisting of cover versions of 'Working Man', 'By-Tor & The Snow Dog', The Analog Kid', 'The Trees', 'La Villa Strangiato', 'Mission', 'Anthem', 'Jacob's Ladder', 'Closer To The Heart', 'Natural Science', 'YYZ', 'Red Barchetta' and 'Freewill', the project was overseen by Terry Brown.

By the autumn, the desire to 'do' Rush again was strong, and writing sessions began at Chalet Studios. Thoughts turned again to a producer, and

Peter Collins was appointed for the second album of his second era. Rough demos of the new material were recorded, and after Christmas, the serious work began in Bearsville Studios, a location recommended by Collins – the first time the band had recorded in America. With the bass and drum tracks completed, the band moved to Reaction Studios for the guitar and vocal parts. Both locations were dogged by particularly bad wintry weather, which didn't ease up at McClear Pathe. Here, the final mixes were overseen by Andy Wallace, who had recently worked with Rage Against The Machine.

The season and climate informed the striking cover design. Syme's image features an Inuksuk (a location marker for the Inuit population) on a bright day in a wintry wilderness. Climbing the rocky object's left leg, thigh and outstretched arm are three tiny, almost indistinct figures. On the rear of the CD booklet insert, three radio transceivers await signals from extraterrestrial life.

The lyric booklet contains more Syme creations, each relating to an individual track. Unusually, the only pictures of the band are three photos taken from their childhood; a teenage Peart is shown smiling broadly behind his drum kit, Lifeson is playing his electric guitar in the family lounge and Lee sits awkwardly outside with a classical guitar on his knees, with the family garden and car as a backdrop.

Test For Echo continues with the guitar-centric, organic rock sound of *Counterparts*. At times seismically heavy, at others relaxed and beautifully melodic, the album is devoid of an overarching lyrical theme. It also sees the welcome return of some of the 'prog-rock' motifs (complex and shifting time signatures, dramatic changes of musical texture and mood) that had been virtually absent from recent releases. The album title was also an implicit question to the fan base. After a three-year break, are you still out there for us? The answer was a resounding 'Yes!'

'Test For Echo' (5.56)

Reflecting the remote beauty of the album cover, 'Test For Echo' begins in an atmosphere of reverb, gentle guitar arpeggios and relaxed vocals. Alternating between the restrained and the savagely brutal attack of the progressively grungy-sounding main riff, the title track is a mini-epic, at times grandiose and overwhelming, at others contemplative and introspective.

Peart and Dubois address the modern times as they see them; everything, and by extension everyone, is a commodity with a financial value. The resultant effect of this is one of 'vertigo' at this intrusion and financial weaponisation by the various mass media dominating our lives.

The central riff is a spectacular display of heaviness, the likes of which we haven't heard for decades. Similarly, the first 'Here we go – vertigo, video, vertigo' section at 1.34 is massive, a dense wall of distorted guitars and vicious bass and drums. As if a gauntlet has been thrown down, Lifeson gives it everything he's got for the opening of the instrumental before the sound relaxes, and he allows space, feel and phrasing to dominate his solo until its powerful climax.

Although there are relatively few musical themes in this impressive six-minute opener, and the pulse and 4/4 time signature remain constant throughout, it's the clever contrast of sounds, dynamics and arrangement that makes the song sound huge, no more so than the main riff bringing it to a tight end.

'Driven' (4.27)

Matching the effective template of *Counterparts,* where 'Stick It Out' bested an impressive first track, 'Driven' is a fast and furious rocker. The main riff powers through the 3/4, 5/4, 3/4 and 4/4 time changes with ease. This pulsating, tense rhythm perfectly complements the lyrical content. It changes very subtly (to 3/4, 5/4, 6/4 and then back to 3/4, 5/4, 3/4, 4/4 again) when underpinning the vocals. All the 'sturm und drang' disappears briefly to be replaced by a bright, strummed acoustic guitar for the refrain: 'But it's my turn to drive'. The full-force band re-appear dramatically as the backing for the chorus: 'Driven to the margin of error ... driven to the edge of a deep dark whole'. The second time this appears, Peart throws in a wonderful, extended drum roll.

Following the second chorus, control of the Wonder Riff ™ is passed to Lee (a triple bass guitar onslaught) as rim shots add tension to Lifeson's distant, sustained screams. This 'calm before the storm' shatters at 2.00 with a short, doom-laden chord sequence that would make Black Sabbath's Tony Iommi proud. This is the basis of the bridge section, which ends with the song's key lyric: 'Driven on by the road to somewhere I've never been'. This part is decorated with many guitars and another fantastic drum fill.

For the final verse and chorus, all thoughts of dynamic and texture shifts are thrown out the window as the song ends with mighty repeats of the Wonder Riff ™ and a heavy, overwrought, screaming guitar solo. It's fantastic stuff!

'Half The World' (3.42)

'Half The World' has a more relaxed, groove-centric feel with plenty of acoustic guitar in the mix for that lighter touch. Intensely melodic throughout, the chorus is the memorable high point of this, the album's shortest song. The only real issue is the distraction caused by the near-constant repetition of the title throughout the track. This technique clouds some thought-provoking words: 'Half the world lives, half the world makes, half the world gives whilst the other half takes' and 'Half the world cries, half the world laughs, half the world tries to be the other half'. The chasm between the rich and poor, the comfortable and the destitute, the satisfied and the desperate never seems to close.

The unexpected instrument in the bridge section (1.44 – 2.13) is a mandola, to which some slap-back delay and reverb have been added. This is a pleasing addition to the final verses, providing a strange, drone-like melody. 'Half The World' is another strong, tuneful and intelligent addition to the collection.

'The Color Of Right' (4.49)

Another heavy and yet strongly melodic rocker with a pop sheen, 'The Color Of Right' shows Rush playing to their many strengths with a dramatic opening that relaxes into an excellent, guitar-based groove. The vocals are top-notch, with the lyrics taking a more personal, relationship-based theme: 'I don't have an explanation for another lonely night'. There is a lovely yearning feel to Lee's voice here and at similar points in the song.

The chorus ups the rhythmic ante with a busier texture, arpeggiated guitars, more involved drums and a subtle ghostly-sounding synth. The bridge ('A quality of justice ... gravity and distance change the color of right') is followed by a short, basic metal-style section of overdriven guitar and off-beat bass drum stabs (2.24 – 2.32). This moves into a simple, tuneful guitar solo, a reprise of the heavier introduction and the return of the chorus. A repeat of Lifeson's straightforward solo brings the track to a sustained close.

'The Color Of Right' is another gem. Its omission from subsequent live albums is a shame, as it is worthy of greater attention for its combination of melody, power and driving arrangement.

'Time And Motion' (5.01)

The outright winner of the award for proggiest rocker on the album, 'Time And Motion' was a rejected track from several years previous, which was then rediscovered, reworked and finally allowed onto an album.

It crams an awful lot into its 40-second introduction: a very heavy guitar, bass and drum riff in 5/4 gives way to a spiralling riff (over a mixture of 12/8 and 10/8) to which some superb organ arpeggios are added. This mutates into a mournful chord sequence in 3/4, which becomes the basis for the verses, where Lee double-tracks his vocals over two octaves.

Lifeson performs a deranged, distorted solo, which is a violent expression of extreme frustration; the guitarist attacks his instrument in what sounds like an attempt to finish it off entirely. His contribution bears little, if any, relation to the musical themes which have preceded it. This is an 'anti-solo' – a compelling demonstration of angst and anger with the making of noise, rather than music, the primary objective. He succeeds in spectacular, if disturbing, fashion.

And then, as if nothing has happened, it's over and the song resumes its relentless course with a section of evocative lyrics, which musically contrasts the heavy with the atmospheric: 'The mighty ocean dances with the moon, the silent forest echoes with the loon' (being a make of bird, rather than a breed of idiot). A reprise of the keyboard introduction with some excellent bass playing carries the song into its final verse and refrain.

'Time And Motion' is another underexposed example of some exceptional heavy, melodic rock with progressive elements fused together to form a composition which is uniquely Rush-ian.

'Totem' (4.58)
This is a brisk, bouncy and melodic tune that drives along with purposeful energy. The chorus is Rush at their most catchy and commercial, whilst still remaining lyrically sincere: 'I believe in what I see, I believe in what I hear, I believe that what I'm feeling changes how the world appears'.

There is plenty of light and shade, with textural and dynamic changes occurring throughout. The happy mood becomes reflective with the 'Angels and demons dancing in my head ... pop culture prophets playing in my ears' section (0.56 – 1.27, and 2.24 – 2.56). In the background, Lifeson creates layer upon layer of chiming, spacious notes, a silvery backdrop to the steady, dark drive of the rhythm section.

The mood darkens further at the three-minute mark with a tasteful, bluesy solo. This stutters into a spacious, haunting section with plenty of feedback replaced by natural harmonics behind the repeated 'Angels and demons inside of me, saviours and Satans all around me'. The song crescendos back into the bright chorus and refrain elements, as the shining wall of guitar sounds decorates the close.

'Dog Years' (4.55)
Another high-energy, tuneful, heavy rocker with elements of rockabilly and even country behind the overdriven guitars in its introduction, 'Dog Years' would work brilliantly as an instrumental, with Lifeson playing the catchy vocal melody.

In a long career of writing, there is always going to be an occasional dip in quality. This one, by any metric other than possibly that of humour, is a low point for Peart. The first verses are prime examples: 'In a dog's life a year is really more like seven, and all too soon a canine will be chasing cars in doggie heaven'. He then equates a dog's life with our own: 'It seems to me as we make our few circles around the sun, we get it backwards and our seven years go by like one'.

The lyric continues in this vein with the metaphor of humans as dogs finally reaching a point. Like dogs, whose sole interests are food, walk and sleep, we 'make our own few circles round the block' and we, too, have 'lost our senses for the higher levels standing on top'. To Peart, too many of us spend too much of our time merely existing, obtaining that which is necessary to survive and possibly progress, rather than consider higher qualities or purposes in our lives.

A quieter, more reflective bridge section follows the second chorus (2.18 – 3.17) and is filled with some gorgeous lower-register guitar arpeggios. This only serves as a tasteful backdrop for more lyrical ridiculousness: 'I'd rather

Above: A promo shot for, most likely, 2004's *Feedback*.

Left: 1984's *Grace Under Pressure* showcased fewer synths, more guitars and some fine songs. (*Anthem*)

Right: The back cover of the live album from the *Grace Under Pressure Tour*, finally released in 2009. (*Anthem*)

Left: The synths assumed control on *Power Windows*. (*Anthem*)

Right: The 'none more red' cover of 1987's *Hold Your Fire.* (*Anthem*)

Left: The band's third live album, *A Show Of Hands*, gave the synth era material another airing. (*Anthem*)

Right: The cover for 1991's *Presto*, which was a mixed bag of an album with a clinical production. (*Anthem*)

Above: As with the 1970s, the 1980s had some dubious fashions.

Below: Alex and Geddy at Wembley Arena in May 1983; note the Steinberger 'headless' bass. (*Pete Still/Redferns*)

Above: 'Thank you and goodnight!' from the *Grace Under Pressure* 1984 live video.

Below: Geddy Lee – bass player, keyboard player and vocalist, sometimes all at the same time.

Left: Alex shredding away in the video for 'Marathon'.

Right: Geddy looking rather guilty of something in the video for 'Mystic Rhythms'.

Left: Aimee Mann, guest vocalist in the video for 'Time Stand Still'.

Above: The trio around the time of *Presto*.

Below: Rupert Hine, the *Presto* producer.

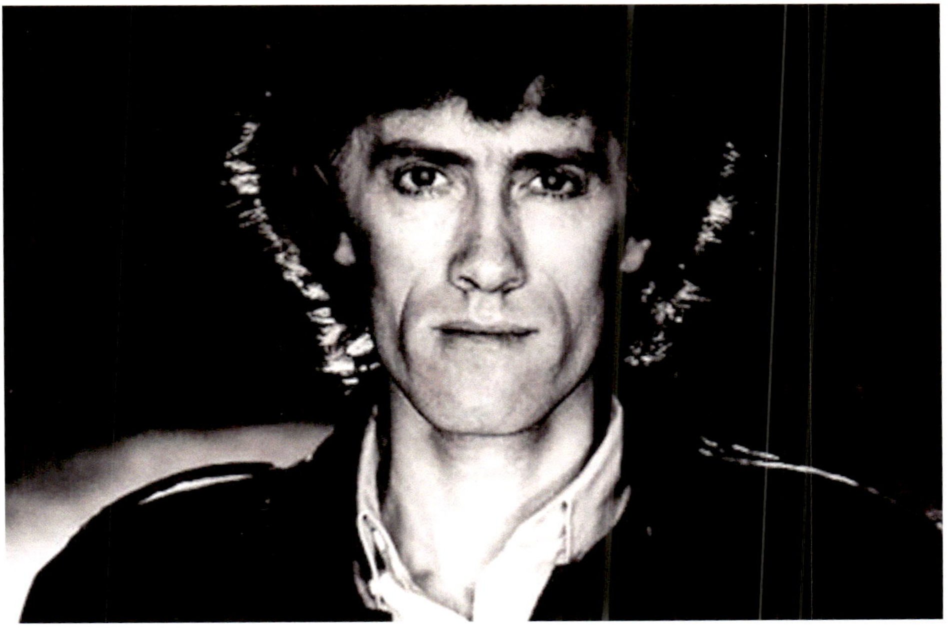

Left: Hugh Syme's award-winning cover for *Roll The Bones*. (*Anthem*)

Right: The *Counterparts* cover, in which the band refuse to be subtle ... (*Anthem*)

Left: *Test For Echo* showcased another striking cover from Syme. (*Anthem*)

Right: At the time, *Different Stages* was thought to be the band's farewell to their legions of fans. (*Anthem*)

Left: And yet, back they came, full of fire and defiance, with 2002's *Vapor Trails*. (*Anthem*)

Right: Rush made a triumphant return to the live arena with the triple-disc *Rush In Rio* (2003). (*Anthem*)

Above: Lee and Lifeson onstage in 1994. (*Ebet Roberts/Redferns*).

Below: And again, this time during the *Test For Echo* tour.

Above: The band's induction into the Rock 'n' Roll Hall of Fame gives Alex an opportunity for comedy..

Below: Another photo from the same event.

Left: *Feedback*'s throwback psychedelic cover signposts this short but great collection of covers of songs that inspired the band in the 1960s. (*Anthem*)

Right: The *R30* anniversary live album, released in 2005, contains two discs of mostly 1980s Rush songs. (*Anthem*)

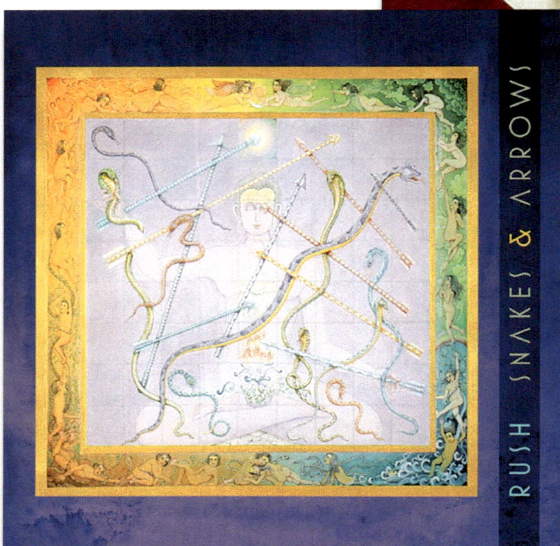

Left: The imaginary board game cover of the 2007 album *Snakes And Arrows*. (*Anthem*)

Right: And the seemingly inevitable live album of the tour that followed in 2008. (*Anthem*)

Left: The *Time Machine* live album featured all of *Moving Pictures*, played sequentially. (*Anthem*)

Right: 2012's *Clockwork Angels* was the band's final studio album and first full-length concept album. (*Roadrunner*)

Above: Peter Collins, producer of four Rush albums between 1986 and 1996.

Below: Nick Raskulinecz, producer of the band's final two studio albums, with Alex looking on.

Above: Not just another gig, this was taken during the final show of the *R40* tour at The Forum, LA. (*Rich Fury/Invision/AP*)

Below: Rush's backbone, Neil Peart, who sadly passed away in 2020. (*Jesse Grant/ Getty Images*)

Left: *Clockwork Angels Tour* featured the intriguing addition of a real string section to some songs. (*Anthem*)

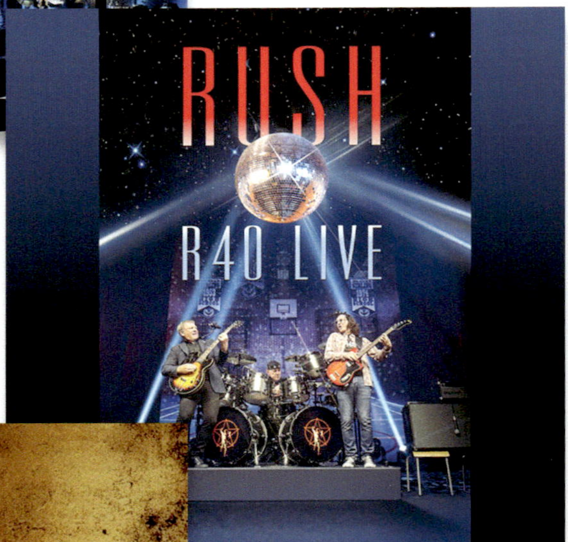

Right: The cover of the band's final live offering, to date at least. (*Anthem*)

Left: The career-spanning, expansive and expensive *R50* package. (*Mercury*)

be a tortoise from Galapagos, or a span of geological time ... than be living in these dog years'.

Taken as a bit of fun, 'Dog Years' is okay, but only okay. It's not good. It's not great. And it doesn't grow on you after repeated listenings. No biscuit for this one.

'Virtuality' (5.44)

The internet was in its infancy when *Test For Echo* was released, and Peart's observations regarding the nature and possibility of electronic communication are backed by another monumental musical slab of Rush at their heavy, proggy best.

The opening riff is an absolute monster, unyielding and remorseless, but there is also room for textural and dynamic variation in the song. The second half of the verse breaks with the intensity as an interesting blend of high-range bass, busy percussion and a repeated distorted guitar motif takes over. The chorus (the rather charming 'Net boy, Net girl, send your impulse round the world, put your message in a modem and throw it in the Cyber Sea') is sung over a vigorously strummed acoustic guitar, backed by some solid but restrained bass and drums.

The song consists of these three musical themes weaving in and out of each other. Whilst there was space for a spectacular Lifeson solo, the opportunity was not taken; he restricts himself to a repeating two-phrase interlude (3.32 – 3.51). As a result, 'Virtuality' becomes too repetitive; some judicious pruning at the rehearsal stage would have produced a better, leaner track.

'Resist' (4.23)

A very pretty-sounding piano and acoustic guitar carry the introduction to this beautiful ballad. The opening lyrics rework Oscar Wilde's oft-quoted saying from his 1892 play 'Lady Windermere's Fan' into 'I can learn to resist anything but temptation', followed by the poignant 'I can learn to co-exist with anything but pain'. Lee sings beautifully here against a wonderfully resonant acoustic guitar.

After the second chorus, Lifeson has a superb, soaring countermelody. Each of the six stanzas (the first and second are repeated as verses five and six) grows in texture, gradually becoming busier and more involving, whilst still maintaining a strong melodic core. At 2.18, everything just drops away, leaving Geddy's isolated voice and a solitary strummed steel-strung guitar.

This is a supremely effective moment. The space freed up by the absence of the other instrumentation adds greater weight to the words: 'You can surrender without a prayer, but never really pray without surrender'. A second guitar and some quiet cymbal work join for the next section: 'You can fight without ever winning, but never win without a fight'.

The introduction and all the other instruments return as the verses are repeated, with several Lees singing in counterpoint with each other. The song concludes with Lifeson's wonderful melody, bringing this excellent ballad to a peaceful end.

'Limbo' (5.28)

In an interview in *Jam!/Showbiz* magazine in October 1986, Peart said:

> Our co-producer, Peter Collins, went out and bought a CD that had a compilation of some funny songs like that. We got to listening to it, thinking how funny it was and decided to put some samples of it in there. That's Igor going 'Goo, mash, goo'. We had to get special permission and pay money and everything.

The third album in a row to offer up a disappointing instrumental; this one should have been left in limbo. It's a mish-mash-up of several differing ideas all linked by a steady mid-tempo pulse, and sadly lacks a defined and engaging central melodic theme. Whilst there are some impressively powerful moments, and the ghostly floating voice of Lee's distant 'aah's appearing at various points are effective, the track sounds like an afterthought. A quick plunder of the 'Discarded Riff' box, a bit of studio finessing and some baffling spoken excerpts from the 1962 novelty pop hit 'Monster Mash' do not make a cohesive musical statement. 'Limbo' is not even much of a display of the band's technical abilities. At five and a half minutes, it's way too long, and *Test For Echo* would be better for its absence.

'Carve Away The Stone' (4.06)

The ancient myth of Sisyphus receives a much-awaited update in a rock setting. Apparently, the self-confident King S was punished for his arrogance by the Gods, who forced him to push a stone all the way to the top of a hill, only for them to send it back to its starting place, forcing the King to do it all again. Endlessly. Those Gods! Such scamps!

Luckily, Peart is on hand to rewrite this tale of hubris into a stoic-based theme for modern times. His reinterpretation pushes the theme in the direction of personal responsibility; chip away at your own stone to 'make the burden lighter, if you must roll that rock alone'. The final chorus concludes with the wry observation: 'Roll away the stone. If you could just move yours, I could get working on my own'.

The opening chord progression suggests an early 1970s incarnation of Rush, with its strident, distorted guitar chords, and the vocal melody soaring above with a bird-like grace. In the chorus, the pulse lurches into 5/4 prior to the vocal melody, which then moves into a mixture of 7/4 and 5/4, serving, on this occasion, to unsettle the music. Despite this, the chorus is cheerfully melodic and catchy, with some crisp guitar arpeggios adding to the lightness of feel.

Pleasingly heavy and full of energy, there's plenty to enjoy in the final track. Whilst Lifeson's solo is not one of his most inspiring, the overall flair and spirit of the individual performances add up to a rocky, upbeat, complex and enjoyable finale.

In *Contents Under Pressure*, Alex summed up the record:

> *Test For Echo* was an extension of what we had been doing for so many years. It was a very enjoyable record to make. There was a nice, even, calm energy to the record, very much like *Moving Pictures*. In fact, we often compare the two in terms of how they were made and how they felt. To my ear, now, 'Test' is a little lighter, a little more shiny, a little more rhythmic ... very rhythmic.

Different Stages – Live (1998)

Personnel:
Alex Lifeson: electric and acoustic guitars,
Geddy Lee: vocals, bass guitar, keyboards
Neil Peart: drums, percussion
Pre-mixed and assembled at Trax Studios, Los Angeles
Produced by James 'Jimbo' Barton
Mixed by James 'Jimbo' Barton and Alex Lifeson
Released: 10 November 1998
Label: Atlantic Records
Chart positions: Canada: 12, US: 35, UK: 121
All music composed by Lee and Lifeson, with lyrics by Peart

Despite the three-year hiatus preceding *Test For Echo*, the band were very much back. The subsequent 68-date tour, the first without a support act, ran from October 1996 to July 1997 and took in 68 dates, was called 'An Evening With ...' and included, for the first time, '2112' in its entirety. Each gig was recorded with a view to releasing a fourth live album. The tour concluded in Ottawa, with the mood within the band triumphant.

On 10 August 1997, everything changed. Peart's only child, Selena, died in a car accident. Subsequently, the health of his wife, Jackie, began to fail, and she died of cancer less than a year later.

For Neil, life stopped, and so did Rush. Nobody felt that any form of band continuation was appropriate but both Geddy and Alex believed that they owed their fans something, as a farewell, if nothing else. In *Contents Under Pressure*, Geddy commented:

> We had been recording material for two tours. We had gathered quite an overwhelming library of material, actually, and, coupled with the discovery of the tapes from 1978, it was just obvious that we needed to put a package together. And in my mind, we were coming up on 25 years as a band; I thought it was an opportune moment to put together a retrospective, in essence, from a live point of view. And because a lot of the responsibility for this project kind of gravitated into my corner, I just kind of decided what the concept was going to be.

In *Chemistry*, Alex remembered the period and the prospects for the band:

> We felt it was unlikely that things would get back together ... and, yes, I think we were okay with it. It was definitely a feeling of sadness. I think that there wasn't a sense of closure with the band, that it was a long history that we had, we'd accomplished a lot of things, and if that's the way it was going to end, then so be it.

The first two CDs of the triple disc *Different Stages – Live* featured songs from recent tours, and covered much of the band's career, whilst the third CD was a recording of a concert at the Hammersmith Odeon, London, on 20 February 1978. The album was dedicated to Jackie and Selena. *All The World's A Stage* was rough and ready, *Exit Stage Left* over-engineered and edited, and *A Show Of Hands,* whilst sounding like a true live album, suffered for its dependency on the band's 'synth era' songs. *Different Stages – Live* is a great blend of high-energy performances. If this were to be a fond farewell from band to fans, it is a satisfying collection to conclude a career. The track listing is as follows, with individual comments reserved for points of difference and interest from the studio version.

Disc 1
'Dreamline' (5.35)
From the fading strains of 'Also Sprach Zarathustra' by Richard Strauss (1864 – 1949), this taut and muscular performance kicks off the best-sounding Rush live album thus far. Lifeson's solo is part improvisatory, being lower-pitched and bluesy, before he goes off on one for the main body of his contribution. There is a rare 'error' when he misfrets the initial high-note scream bend prior to the final choruses, but this is how live albums should be, trading perfection for moments of 'on-the-edge' musical abandon.

'Limelight' (4.33)

'Driven' (5.17)
After the second chorus, we have a rare bass solo section (1.39 – 2.27) based around the introductory riff with some effective use of a delay pedal and pauses. At 2.28, Lifeson eases into his solo over the bass, and by 2.41, the trio are back on familiar ground.

'Bravado' (6.23)
'Animate' (6.29)

'Show Don't Tell' (5.29)
The original fade is replaced with a slowed-down reprise of the introduction, with Peart pulverising his drums to close.

'The Trees' (5.29)
The end section of the song has an extended pastoral texture with plenty of gentle improvisation from both Lifeson and Lee as they wander about their fretboards. For good measure, the sounds of birds, a dog and, erm, a cow are also heard. Of course.

'Nobody's Hero' (5.01)

'Closer To The Heart' (5.13)
The extended jam at the song's end is now a key part of the stage performances.

'2112'
This is the first time the career-making track has made a complete appearance on a live album. Given that two decades had passed by the time this recording was made, the decision to tune the instruments down a tone (from E to D) assists Lee with the extremes of the vocal range, and also makes the entire song even heavier than it was before. As a consequence, I feel it deserves a full review.

I: 'Overture' (4.33)
This fact is immediately emphasised in the storming rendition of the 'Overture', where Lee's bass fills are of especial note, and an enthusiastic crowd are well in on the act. The brief vocals at the end ('And the meek shall inherit the earth') are very much the only point of peace before the onslaught continues....

II: 'The Temples Of Syrinx' (2.20)
What was already an intensely aggressive song receives a spectacular sonic makeover. Astonishingly heavy, each player is on fire here, with Lee in fine voice, even if it is right at the very top of his range.

III: 'Discovery' (4.17)
This is an opportunity for Lifeson to display his consummate improvisatory skills, which he deploys to great effect here. Rather than starting with the retuning of the long-lost guitar, he indulges in some Celtic-style drone-based creativity with a beautiful tone. At 1.37, he returns to the studio origins with Lee's matchless vocals, creating just the right mood. This soon blends into...

IV: 'Presentation' (3.40)
...'Presentation', where the window-shattering heaviness returns, and Lee's vocals are astonishing, rising above the sound and fury of the band. The end-of-song solo shows Lifeson at the other extreme of his guitar sound: vicious, agonised and so alive.

V: 'Oracle/The Dream' (1.49)
The opening arpeggiated chords feature a modulation effect where each individual string sounds out of tune with itself, whilst still harmonising with the rest of the chord. It's a weird and disconcerting tone that, whilst obviously intended, doesn't fit well with the rest of the quieter sections of the piece. This is soon trampled over with the overbearing weight of the power trio, where once again the vocals are superb.

VI: 'Soliloquy' (2.08)
Here, Lifeson uses a more familiar and traditional chorus effect for his introduction. The subsequent agonised vocals and pain-ridden, distorted guitar solo are perfect foils for each other.

VII: 'Grand Finale' (2.37)
More heaviness of the most fabulous kind rounds off things triumphantly. It sounds like Lee and Lifeson are having the time of their lives, backed by Peart's ominous onslaughts. A long note consisting mainly of feedback and delay rounds things off after the 'Attention all planets' pronouncement.

Disc 2
'Test For Echo' (6.16)
'The Analog Kid' (5.14)
'Freewill' (5.36)

'Roll The Bones' (5.58)
The rap section would have been a good opportunity for one of Lifeson's improvised spoken-word routines, which would frequently appear in live performances of 'La Villa Strangiato'.

'Stick It Out' (4.43)
'Resist' (4.43)
'Leave That Thing Alone' (4.46)

'The Rhythm Method' (8.20)
The full solo, previously heard in edited form on *A Show Of Hands*, is another tour-de-force demonstration of what one man can do with a set of drums and some electronic percussion. When you can make a drum solo sound interesting to non-drummers, that is genuine talent. Peart does not indulge in the 'call and response' audience participation, which many heavy rock drummers use as an essential part of the ritual. His natural musicality and desire to create rather than just impress means we are listening to a considered, complex and yet accessible composition; a demonstration of intelligence, phenomenal technique, great imagination, and a determination not to just 'go out there and do the same thing again.'

This is not to say there aren't many other great drummers out there who have similar skills, but Peart's emergence as an astonishing rock drummer during the 1970s, when drum solos were an inevitable and unavoidable part of the concert experience, shows that he was a pioneer of creativity.

'Natural Science' (8.05)
'The Spirit Of Radio' (5.00)
'Tom Sawyer' (5.19)

'YYZ' (5.26)
At 4.22, the band suddenly lurch into a brief excerpt from the middle of 'Cygnus X-1' before returning to finish things off with the final four notes of 'YYZ'.

Disc 3

The third CD of the package is a concert at the Hammersmith Odeon, London, on 20 February 1978. Intended for a radio broadcast which never transpired, it's an audio snapshot of the band on their *Kings* tour, and it's a fascinating listen. This 'bonus' disc is, of course, absolute aural catnip for fans who first discovered the band in the 1970s.

The recording was engineered by Terry Brown, and, given the length of time the tapes had remained unattended, the sound is remarkably good. It is a warts-and-all experience, and is all the better for it. This is the genuine live recording; no re-touching, no editing, no drop-ins. This is a historical document of just how good Rush were at transporting their carefully crafted rock music onto the stage with electrifying results.

'Bastille Day' (5.08)
'By-Tor & The Snow Dog' (4.59)
'Xanadu' (12.32)
'A Farewell To Kings' (5.53)
'Something For Nothing' (4.01)

'Cygnus X-1' (10.23)
Lee inserts pauses in his first quiet vocals ('Invisible to tele ... scopic eye, In ... finity, the star that ... would not die'). It's probably me, but when listening to this, I always imagine *Star Trek*'s William Shatner voicing these lyrics. 'Captain Kirk sings the music of Rush' – now, that's an album I'd pay good money to hear.

'Anthem' (4.47)

'Working Man' (4.00)
Lee amusingly changes the lyrics of the second verse from 'ice-cold beer' to 'Watney's Red Barrel', a happily now-long-defunct English beer, the taste of which probably contravened the terms of the European Convention on Human Rights. The instrumental is cut short at the end of the simultaneous 'octave riff' section, segueing straight into 'Fly By Night'.

'Fly By Night' (2.04)
'In The Mood' (3.34)
'Cinderella Man' (5.09)

Vapor Trails (2002)

Personnel:
Alex Lifeson: electric and acoustic guitars, mandola
Geddy Lee: vocals, bass guitar
Neil Peart: drums, percussion
Recorded at Reaction Studios, Toronto, between August and December 2001
Produced by Rush and Paul Northfield
Released: 14 May 2002
Label: Atlantic Records
Chart positions: Canada: 3, US: 6, UK: 38
All music composed by Lee and Lifeson, with lyrics by Peart

A grief-stricken Peart took himself motorcycling across Canada and America, ending up in Mexico, trying to leave his past behind. His excellent book *Ghost Rider* does not dwell on his tragedies, but is a fascinating read, and indicates that the drummer's ability as a prose writer matched his skills as a lyricist. In his book, Neil opened up about the double tragedies:

> I didn't really have a reason to carry on. I had no interest in life, work or the world beyond, but unlike Jackie, who had surely willed her death, I seemed to be armoured with some kind of survival instinct, some inner reflex that held to the conviction that 'something will come up'. Because of some strength (or flaw) of character, I never seemed to question 'why' I should survive, but only 'how' – though that was certainly a big enough question to deal with at the time.

Lee spent a lot of time writing and recording some of his own songs with Ben Mink, the violinist who had played the anguished solo on 'Losing It' (*Signals*). On 14 November 2000, Lee's debut solo album, *My Favourite Headache*, finally appeared. It is a very different venture compared to Lifeson's darkly aggressive *Victor*. Lee's melodic skills give us a more accessible collection, which is well worth a listen. Two additional 'lost' tracks were made available to download in 2024.

Over time, Peart came to realise that his self-imposed exile was not working for him. A chance meeting with a tarot reader gave him an astonishingly accurate reading of what his future held, and also set Rush in motion again. By mid-1999, Peart had tentatively returned to a drum stool. It was the band's official 'snapper', Andrew McNaughton, who introduced him to another photographer, Carrie Nuttall, in Los Angeles in November 1999. The couple were married in September 2000 in Montecito, near Santa Barbara, and decided to live in California.

Shortly before the wedding, Peart knew that he needed to return to Rush. By the end of 2000, the band were officially back together. Paul Northfield was chosen as producer, and gradually, a new album was created. Wanting

the new project to be full of energy and intensity, the band and producer overworked the recording process to the extent that the finished results were not to everybody's liking. Despite the fact that it was the first of the band's albums since 1975's *Caress Of Steel* not to use synthesisers, Lee and Lifeson decided to overdub many layers of heavily overdriven guitar and bass to make the songs sound as full and energetic as possible. In the final mix, they also included several of the original 'jam' recordings the pair had made when putting their initial musical ideas together into the final songs. The net result was 'too much of too much'. When the then-fashionable process of high-level mastering was used, the overall result sounded overly distorted and not the pleasingly powerful experience that this fan was hoping for.

In an interview with *Classic Rock* magazine in January 2025, Lifeson said that the 'phoenix from the flames' emergence of Rush was like a rebirth:

> It changed how we worked as songwriters ... how we interacted. That album was a turning point. We are two very different songwriters and arrangers. I'm somewhat more immediate and instinctive, whereas (Geddy) is more focused and methodical. These are primary personality traits that contributed to our partnership and the synergy of our efforts. I remember that for the first few weeks in the studio for that record, we didn't play a single note; we talked, really.

He continued:

> Then, we started writing; it took a couple of months just to clear the cobwebs. Most of the stuff we originally wrote was us just going through the motions; I think a lot of it sounded dated. And then we took a break, and when we came back, the machine started rolling and the record took on a life of its own.

Vapor Trails was finally released after an 18-month incubation period. It was a record that sounded like nothing Rush had released before. In place of any keyboards, choirs of Lees, a vocal layering technique Lee had fully developed on *My Favourite Headache*, provided plenty of additional texture.

The cover, a blazing fireball against a black-and-white background, is an excellent image for the music; passionate, full of fire and attack. The inner artwork includes images of tarot cards for each song, chosen by Peart to represent his lyrics. In *Contents Under Pressure*, bassist and guitarist reflected on this period of the band's history. Geddy:

> It's one of my favourite records that we've ever done. There's something about that record that is really raw and really passionate. And in some ways, even though it's nothing like it, it has a kind of focus that reminds me of *2112*, in a way, just in its kind of 'balls-to-the-wall' attitude, the playing. It's a real album of playing out.

Alex:

> Obviously, having gone through what Neil went through, and what we all went through, it was definitely going to impact where this record was going to go. To me, the record is very optimistic. It's all about recovery and about hope, about a future, rebirth and moving forward. There are some dark moments, some sad moments, but generally it's really about those things I just mentioned. And the course that the lyrics take to get that message across covers a lot of ground, from a very personal experience to a more universal representation of it.

Fan and band dissatisfaction with the overall sound of the original album led to another first. *Vapor Trails* was remixed by David Bottril and reissued, with altered cover art, on 27 September 2013. It is a much better listen with greater clarity between the competing instruments, whilst still maintaining the intensity of the original release. *Vapor Trails* is almost entirely devoid of guitar solos. It was a 'back-to-basics' attempt to discover what Rush now meant, and what fresh music they could create together again. In an interview with *Guitar International*, Alex said:

> From the heavy stuff to the more melodic stuff, it was a very fragile representation of the band. In mastering, unfortunately, it was a contest, and everything was mastered too high, and it crackles, and it spits, and it just crushes everything. All the dynamics get lost, especially anything that had an acoustic guitar in it.

In *Contents Under Pressure*, he spoke about the new dynamic within the band:

> How time has affected a band like us, I can't really say, because it's not just time. It's not just the longevity; it's the impact of what happens in that time. Really, all of us questioned whether or not we'd make another record, if we would ever work again. When all this happened, the band was the very last thing on our minds. I mean, it just didn't seem appropriate to even think about it. Music's about celebration, and there was no feeling of celebration at that time. It was circle the wagons and help as much as you can.

'One Little Victory' (5.08)

A thunder of drums and a cavalcade of guitar and bass riffage lay the band's cards on the table. There's a full minute of this high-octane blast before the vocals appear, riding out over a swaggering groove. This is the sound of a rejuvenated band, full of confidence and attitude, a celebration of life over death.

This fan was uncertain as to what to expect given Peart's recent history. For this song, his chosen stance was, perhaps inevitably, one of defiance and perseverance, especially with the chorus: 'Celebrate the moment, as it turns into one more. Another chance at victory, another chance to score'. The combination of music, vocals and lyrics is potent and uplifting.

'One Little Victory' is Rush rocking hard and sounding fantastic as a result. Lee's voice soars, Lifeson's gritty guitars provide an uncompromising backing and Peart is putting everything into his drumming. In the remixed version of the album, Lifeson's high-energy solo (3.59 – 4.36) cuts through the melee, the track pounding its way to an abrupt end.

'Ceiling Unlimited' (5.28)

If anything, 'Ceiling Unlimited' is even better. Another rocker which powers along at an unrelenting pace, greater attention is paid to dynamics here. The lyrics bite: 'The slack jaw gaze of true profanity feels more like surrender than defeat. If culture is the curse of the thinking class', being an especially good couplet, amongst many.

The chorus is one of the most affecting sections of music in the band's entire catalogue, leading into the repeated refrain 'Winding like an ancient river, the time is now again'. Powerfully melodic, addictive and, above all, transcendent in its ability to lift the listener, it is a testament to the band's seemingly endless capacity for reinvention.

Peart indulges in some humour with the lines 'I rest my case, at least my vanity' in the fourth verse before the magnificent chorus returns. The instrumental section keeps the needles in the red, with Lee providing some high-octave bass pyrotechnics before Lifeson's intense, although too short, distorted solo. The final section has a further chorus and a fade-out over the refrain being sung by alternating Lees: 'Hope is like an endless river, the time is now again'.

'Ghost Rider' (5.40)

The mood turns pensive as Peart addresses, in a universal style, the tragedies he has endured. Appropriately enough, the lyrics for this song are printed on the page of the CD booklet, opposite a painting of the lyricist.

The opening music is quieter, spacious, over a pulsing bass, the guitar tinged with overdrive as Lee gives superb voice to the words. The song builds into a solid, mid-tempo groove where drums, bass, guitars and vocals are beautifully balanced. A new section increases the heaviness, and a memorable vocal melody appears under the lyrics 'Keep on riding north and west, then circle south and east. Show me beauty, but there is no peace, for the ghost rider'.

The power builds inexorably into the next section ('Shadows on the road behind ... nothing can stop you now') until the sound drops away suddenly into a repeat of the quiet introduction and a further verse. The second section is reprised with more excellent lyrics reflecting Peart's extended road trip across thousands of miles and sights, a relentless attempt to escape the awful reality that had engulfed him.

The instrumental section finds a distant guitar solo sneaking into the mix amidst the choral vocalisations and the combined assault of bass and drums. This is the song's coda with the repeated refrain 'Nothing can stop you now' echoing around the stereo channels, the song coming to a sudden stop.

If any track was deserving of a fade, 'Ghost Rider' is it. Perhaps the point of the direct ending was to maintain the energy of the album, or to suggest that, even when one is motoring along, something unexpected can suddenly occur, disturbing our equilibrium.

'Peaceable Kingdom' (5.23)

A heartfelt wish for a world where people can live together, the tarot card illustration for 'Peaceable Kingdom' has a close association with the terrorist attacks on the World Trade Centre in September 2001. Peart contrasts those who wish for a better future for everyone with the 'billion other dealers' who 'are slipping past our guards' and 'a billion other teachers are teaching them how to burn'.

'Peaceable Kingdom' is another very heavy song, this time at a steadier tempo, with Lee's various vocals decorating the mix throughout. A brief, pummelling section of power chords crossing over 3/4, 4/4, 3/4 and 5/4 time suddenly opens out into a more relaxed feel for the chorus. The multi-time-signatured section reappears for a tarot-based section of words: 'Justice against The Hanged Man, Knight of Wands against the hour. Swords against the Kingdom, time against The Tower'.

The contrasts between the melodic chorus and the overwhelming musical weight of the rest of the song are highly effective, especially with the reprise of the 'Tarot/Time Signature' section. Bereft of a guitar solo – although benefiting from a superb, low-down, funky distorted riff, which comes into its own at 3.20 – 'Peaceable Kingdom' works through this balance of power and melody and another catchy refrain. Four songs in, and a reborn Rush are in fine fettle.

'The Stars Look Down' (4.28)

The song title comes from the 1935 novel by A J Cronin (1896 – 1981). In this up-tempo and positive-sounding rocker, Peart takes a more pessimistic view of the role of fortune in life. We may feel we have control of our destinies, but our lives are completely at the mercy of fate. Essentially, the lyricist suggests the existence of an omnipresent, complacent God, a being that allows tragedies to occur without a care for the consequences. And, of course, there has to be an autobiographical element to consider.

Musically, 'The Stars Look Down' has a more varied sonic palette. There is space for greater changes of dynamics and texture, especially with the chorus ('What is the meaning of this? ... What are you trying to do? ... Was it something I said?'), where some intriguing backwards recorded instrumentation gives the music a late 1960s psychedelic feel. The presence of the mandola and acoustic guitar brings some welcome relief amidst all the power and glory of the surrounding riffage.

The song's theme, helplessness in the face of life's challenges, is captured with the killer couplet 'Like the rat in a maze who says 'Watch me choose my own direction", whilst the subsequent instrumental is an impressive wall of musical noise. This lapses back into the acoustic backing of the chorus, where the backwards guitars rear their headstocks again. The song drifts to an end with another chorus and repeated 'And the stars look down' over the acoustic instruments and more reversed guitars.

'How It Is' (4.05)

A gorgeous blend of 12-string guitar and mandola gives this poppy-sounding track a light and breezy air. This suddenly breaks into a funky riff-fuelled rocker driven along at a brisk pace before relaxing back into a half-tempo feel for the chorus. The contrast between the gritty verses and languid chorus is again effective, with Peart positing the view that when life feels dark and tough-going, such feelings are not permanent, no matter how unbelievable that concept may feel at the time.

The mood becomes lighter still after the second chorus at 2.38, with the encouragement to overcome temporary troubles – 'Foot upon the stair, shoulder to the wheel' – concluding with the couplet, 'You can't tell yourself not to care, you can't tell yourself what to feel'. The major key of the accompanying music provides a hopeful backdrop as the song builds into repeated choruses to close.

'Vapor Trail' (4.57)

The (almost) title track replaces hope with a bleak despair. Peart ponders the fleeting nature of our existence and the things we consider important in our lives. His words have a darkly poetic quality to them: 'The sun is turning black, the world is turning grey. All the stars fade from the night, the oceans drain away' and 'Silence killed the songbirds, stilled by the killing frost. Forests burn to ashes, everything is lost' being striking examples.

Musically, the track is less depressing with a pleasing blend of 12-string guitars decorating the relatively simple opening chord sequence (B minor, G major, E minor, D major, A major). The sound becomes more brutal for the chorus, where an overdriven guitar and the choir of Lees are backed by a blitz of drums and a busy bass pattern. A short instrumental section at 2.55 has long, sustained lines from Lifeson giving way to another hard-hitting chorus before the song finishes with a final minor chord.

'Secret Touch' (6.34)

Another song that shifts between soft, ambient sections and blistering hard rock, 'Secret Touch' is outstanding. The lyrics once again support the stoic approach to life. The 'secret touch' refers to the occasional connections Peart allowed himself in his grief-stricken journey with the very few people who were close to him.

Musically, it is an absolute blast. The band power through the song with an attack and spirit that is sometimes astonishing; if the listener wants a single example of just how on fire the reunited trio are, try this track. One high point is the climactic line 'A gentle hand, a secret touch on the heart' (2.31 – 2.39), where Lee's voice goes stratospheric against the bombardment of a spectacularly heavy chord sequence. This artistic brutality just doesn't let up, culminating in a hard-edged funk riff section at 4.00, which moves into another chorus. At 5.10, the music calms back down to a reprise of the introduction. This turns into an extended jam section between the trio.

'Earthshine' (5.38)

The first song to emerge from the band's reunion as a working unit, 'Earthshine' had a troubled gestation. Peart's lyrics remained unaltered, but Lifeson and Lee battled to find music to work best with the words. What they came up with was well worth the effort. Backed by another sensational riff and a wonder-groove, Peart describes an astronomical phenomenon: 'On certain nights, when the angles are right, and the moon is a slender crescent, its circle shows in a ghostly glow of earthly luminescence'.

As the music moves onwards, it becomes more rhythmically complex, passing through two bars of 3/4 and a single bar of 5/4, a sequence which is repeated four times. The catchily tuneful chorus also features myriad time signature pyrotechnics; this beat displacement technique doesn't disrupt the rocking flow of the music one iota.

For the second verse, the astral phenomena become a metaphor for how much, or in reality how little, other people see of one's true persona. Following the second chorus, the instrumental features a sequence of a bar of 7/4 then 4/4, which is played four times. Over this complex groove, some sustained distortion from Lifeson provides an eerie, harmonised howl that continues as the music relaxes into 4/4, his solo reaching a fantastic apex with its final note.

The third verse expands the metaphor further, the lyricist needing others to inspire him, in the same way the moon cannot be seen without the sun's light. 'Earthshine' was warmly received when it became a feature of the rejuvenated band's live set list, and rightly so.

'Sweet Miracle' (3.40)

The shortest song on the album, 'Sweet Miracle' has a lighter feel with a superb vocal performance. Another hopeful lyric is underpinned by a syncopated, funky guitar riff and a positive, strum-along style. The track describes Peart's mental state in the aftermath of the death of his family, the chorus marvelling at how love can bring a person back into life. Highly melodic and relentlessly uplifting musically, 'Sweet Miracle' is a welcome change of mood after the intensity of what has gone before.

'Nocturne' (4.49)

Opening with an impressive power-trio assault, a buzzy bass soon takes centre stage for Peart's musings on the nature of dreams (memorably described in the second verse as taking place 'behind the curtain of sleeping eyes') as he 'sets off on a night-sea journey without memory or desire, drifting through lost latitudes with no compass or chart'.

The sound becomes very aggressive for the chorus ('temporary madness ... a voice in the wilderness ... unconscious realisation'), the song lapsing back into a half-time, funk-flavoured feel for the verses. In its very busy and very loud sections, 'Nocturne' has everything turned up way past 11, and it's a bruising experience, even with the newfound clarity of the remix.

Despite its lyrical strength and committed performance, 'Nocturne' fails to hold the attention in the same way as 'Secret Touch' or 'Earthshine'. It's the first song of the album not to engage this listener. If anything, the arrangement and production of this song are just too much for the ears. And the source material is a step down from the high-quality compositions which have preceded it.

'Freeze' (6.21)

And this is the second. Subtitled 'Part IV of 'Fear'', 'Freeze' is the album's least accessible or enjoyable track. The trilogy from the 1980s is joined by this composition, and it is a jarring 'mood piece', impressive from a technical standpoint, but not involving emotionally.

Settling into 6/4 time (with bars of 5/4 and 7/4 thrown in for good measure) for the evocative first verse ('The city crouches, steaming in the early morning half light. The sun is still a rumour and the night is still a threat...'), the song becomes more 'Rush-like' with a heroic-sounding distorted guitar section over a 5/4 beat. The music is taut, claustrophobic and eminently suited to the song's subject matter; given the option of 'fight or flight' in stressful situations, some animals merely 'freeze'.

However, like the sun breaking through clouds, 'Freeze' suddenly warms up, becoming much more melodic at 1.39. Chiming guitars, a steady 4/4 beat and a major-key backing are all at odds with the dark lyrics ('Coiled for the spring or caught like a creature in the headlights ...') and what has gone before. This feels like two separate songs pushed together to make one big one.

The musical tension soon returns, and for me, this is complexity for its own sake. Whilst the use of unusual time signatures supports the tense nature of the lyrics, 'Freeze' rarely feels like it's anything other than an exercise in revisiting old prog tropes. Lifeson's contributions are largely a display of the harsh-sounding effects and noises that can be achieved with a distorted electric guitar. The choir of Lees, whilst providing colour in the instrumental section, merely add to the collection of kitchen sinks that the band have managed to crowbar into this strange, unsettling and unsatisfying track.

'Out Of The Cradle' (5.03)

After a couple of missteps, balance is restored for the final track, a rocker pulsing with energy and another song of hope, neatly book-ending the collection with 'One Little Victory'.

Lee is in fine voice, there's plenty of prominent guitar in the mix and Peart propels the trio forward into the top-flight chorus: 'Surge of energy, the breath of love is electricity. Maybe time is a bird in flight, endlessly rocking. Here we come – out of the cradle, endlessly rocking'. The sense of defiance, which has been a theme of the album, is neatly encapsulated as the band soar away, looking forward to their next project.

The pace lessens at 2.34 with a half-tempo section featuring some vocal gymnastics, an unusual-sounding guitar and a crescendo into another chorus. This is a band renewed, refreshed and ready for whatever the future has to throw at them as they forge their own unique path through the musical firmament. It is an excellent finale to an album that many fans believed would never materialise.

Rush In Rio (2003)

Personnel:
Alex Lifeson: electric and acoustic guitars,
Geddy Lee: vocals, bass guitar, keyboards
Neil Peart: drums, percussion
Recorded at Maracanã Stadium, Rio de Janeiro, Brazil, on 19 October, 27 September and 23 November 2002
Pre-mixed and Assembled at Trax Studios, Los Angeles
Produced by James 'Jimbo' Barton
Mixed by James 'Jimbo' Barton and Alex Lifeson
Released: 21 October 2003
Label: Atlantic Records
Chart positions: Canada: not applicable, US: 33, UK: 139
All music composed by Lee and Lifeson, with lyrics by Peart, except 'O Baterista', music by Peart

Following the success of *Vapor Trails*, thoughts turned to the elephant in the arena – a tour. A proposed 38-date jaunt around the United States and Canada, with the option of some overseas dates, soon increased to 67 shows. The tour opened in Hartford, Connecticut, on 28 June 2002 to a sold-out arena and a rapturous reception – this would be replicated everywhere Rush appeared. Some concerts were planned in uncharted territory for the trio – South America. Record audiences of 25,000 in Porto Alegre, 60,000 in São Paolo and 44,000 at the show in Rio de Janeiro proved to the band just how popular they still were, even in a country they had never played before.

Disc 1
'Tom Sawyer' (5.05)
'Distant Early Warning' (4.51)
'New World Man' (4.05)
'Roll The Bones' (6.15)
'Earthshine' (5.44)

'YYZ' (4.57)
'The Pass' (4.52)
'Bravado' (6.19)

'The Big Money' (6.03)
The final section is a total joy as all three play their hearts out until a bizarre excerpt from *The Simpsons* ('Doh' (Homer), 'A deer' (Lisa), 'A female deer' (Marge)) hastens the huge power chord ending. Magnificent!

'The Trees' (5.12)
'Freewill' (5.49)

'Closer To The Heart' (3.05)
'Natural Science' (8.35)

Disc 2
'One Little Victory' (5.32)
'Driven' (5.23)
'Ghost Rider' (5.37)
'Secret Touch' (7.00)
'Dreamline' (5.11)
'Red Sector A' (5.17)
'Leave That Thing Alone' (4.59)

'O Baterista' (8.54)
Another tour de force, showcasing Peart's talents as a drummer. 'O Baterista' (Spanish and Portuguese for 'The Drummer') was nominated for the best rock instrumental performance category at the Grammy Awards in 2005, and concludes with an excerpt from 'One O'Clock Jump', written by Count Basie and recorded by The Buddy Rich Band, to much audience acclaim.

'Resist'
Just two men, with an acoustic guitar each, playing a beautiful rearrangement of the excellent ballad from *Test For Echo*. Despite the vast venue and huge crowd, this song has a lovely, intimate quality. The crowd provide additional vocals, clapping along to this first-class re-imagining of the song.

'2112' (6.52)
It's not the song in its entirety. This version, and most subsequent live performances, consists of just 'Overture' and 'The Temples Of Syrinx'.

Disc 3
'Limelight' (4.29)
'La Villa Strangiato' (10.05)
'The Spirit Of Radio' (5.29)

'By-Tor & The Snow Dog' (4.35)
The first of the encores, 'By-Tor' is a real surprise, the band seemingly determined to represent as many stages of their career as they can fit into this concert. 'By-Tor' blasts along, having the time of its life after so long in sonic captivity, the band careening through '7/4 War Furore'. The atmospheric 'Aftermath' is then replaced by the introduction to ...

'Cygnus X-1' (3.12)
Ignoring the spacey sound effects and the opening monologue, this is an incredibly powerful performance of this complex piece, stopping short just

before the first vocals, as Lifeson cranks out the monstrous riff of ...

'Working Man' (5.48)
This anthem for the Everyman almost buckles under its own sonic weight. By now, the crowd are in a state of near rapture. Lifeson cuts loose in the frenetic solo section, and the song builds to a monumental ending.

'Between Sun & Moon' (4.51)
Recorded at the Phoenix Cricket Pavilion, Arizona, on 27 September 2002.

'Vital Signs' (4.59)
Recorded at the Colisee, Quebec City, on 19 October 2002.

Feedback (2004)

Personnel:
Geddy Lee: bass guitar, vocals
Alex Lifeson: guitars (electric, acoustic, mandola)
Neil Peart: drums and cymbals
Recorded at Reaction Studios, Toronto, between March and April 2004
Produced by David Leonard and Rush
Released: 29 June 2004
Label: Atlantic Records
Chart positions: Canada: 5, US: 19, UK: 19

A tour to commemorate Peart's arrival in 1974, and promoted as the band's 30th anniversary, was arranged with European dates included. Rush found themselves in the unusual position of having no new material to present on stage. The idea of a covers album was floated, with the emphasis on the music that had inspired the trio as teenagers.

Producer David Leonard (who had acted in the same role for *My Favourite Headache* for Lee) oversaw the project at Phase 1 Studios in Toronto in the spring of 2004. The short album (all 27 minutes of it) was recorded in just a fortnight. Lifeson and Lee insisted that all the chosen songs should feature as much of the guitar 'feedback' as possible, hence the album title. The cover sports a splendid late-1960s psychedelic poster-themed image, listing the songs underneath the 'headline act' of Rush. The eight tracks are not presented in the running order on the CD. This is the sound of the band letting their hair down, as they pay serious tribute to the music that influenced them.

'Summertime Blues' (Cochran/Capeheart) (3.52)
Opening with a squall of ... erm ... feedback, which quickly mutates into a 'Riff Of Unknown Origin' (actually it's lifted from the Blue Cheer version of the track, itself released in 1968, becoming a hit single), Eddie Cochran's outstanding 1958 song is, in Rush's collective hands, given a thoroughly modern makeover. Very heavy, very powerful and committed, this is Rush attacking their influences with the same professionalism as their own material.

However, there is still space for invention in this homage. Instead of the final line of the original's first verse ('My boss says 'No dice son, you gotta work late"), we are treated to a wall of riffing guitars in its place (and listen out for the 'Yeah' of pure joy just audible in the background). This trick is also deployed in the second and third verses, where the lines 'Uh, you can't use the car 'cause you didn't work a lick' and 'I'd like to help you son, but you're too young to vote' are replaced with a frantic bass solo and a spectacular, phased roll around the drums, respectively. A Lifeson solo leads to a key change from A to B major for the third verse, the song concluding with a reprise of the Blue Cheer riff and a big power chord ending, with Peart seemingly trying to destroy his drum kit.

'Heart Full Of Soul' (Gouldman) (2.52)
The Yardbirds' 1965 single, written by Graham Gouldman, who would later go on to be 25% of the original 10cc, is given a sonic upgrade here. Trails of feedback begin and end the track, with Lifeson dispensing with the sitar tone of the original. Rush's version is slower, whilst keeping a pleasing, strummed acoustic guitar at the front of the mix, and the high-energy rolling rhythm of the chorus is maintained. The vocal harmonies of the chorus are simpler than The Yardbirds' recording, and Lifeson adds multiple sustaining guitar lines in the background to fill out the texture.

'For What It's Worth' (Stills) (3.30)
Written by Steven Stills, who would later be the Stills of Crosby, Stills, Nash & Young, this 1966 single was first recorded by Buffalo Springfield. Rush's version is similar in tone and mood, with the distinctive guitar harmonics and Lee's relaxed vocal style being close, but not identical, to the original. Atmospheric, sustained electric guitar lines float over the acoustic accompaniment, Lifeson providing suitable psychedelic touches throughout, especially with his solos.

'The Seeker' (Townsend) (3.27)
A welcome change of pace and mood, 'The Seeker' is energetic, loud and proud. The Who's 1970 single gets a joyous reinterpretation here, being very slightly faster and considerably more aggressive. Losing the occasional mandolin and piano touches of the original, and relying upon the guitar, bass and drums backbone of the rock trio, adds to this version, with Lifeson really 'digging in' for his solo, and Lee's voice matching Daltrey's delivery.

'Mr Soul' (Young) (3.51)
Another Buffalo Springfield song, this time from the Young of Crosby, Stills, Nash & Young, Rush's take is slower and less anguished, whilst still retaining the psychedelic flourishes of the 1967 original.

'Seven And Seven Is' (Lee) (2.53)
This Lee is Arthur of the group Love, who released the song as a single in July 1966. Rush maintain the speed and ferocity of the track, but with a much better vocalist, as Geddy Lee double-tracks the words with himself. Fortunately, the nuclear explosion sound effect and weak blues fade-out of the original are dispensed with as the trio power their way through the song to a frenetic end.

'Shape Of Things' (McCarty, Relf, Samwell-Smith) (3.16)
The Yardbirds' first chart hit, released in 1966, gives Lifeson an opportunity to ape Jeff Beck's innovative guitar work in this slightly slower rendition of one

of the 1960s' most influential songs. The final section is tumultuous, where just about every weapon in Rush's arsenal is thrown at the thunderous conclusion.

'Crossroads' (Johnson) (3.27)
'The Cross Road Blues', to give the classic song its full title, was originally just one man, a bottleneck slide and an acoustic guitar when it appeared in 1937. Receiving an electric overhaul by Cream for their 1968 album *Wheels Of Fire*, and shortened to just 'Crossroads', it is this 'cover of a cover' that Rush turn their attentions to. This 'Crossroads' is a meaty, energetic affair, with Lifeson, especially, having the time of his life as he attempts to break a set of strings and demolish a wah-wah pedal simultaneously for his solo. The final section of this reverential and yet still individual reinterpretation sees the band powering through to the climax – a suitable close to an unexpected and highly enjoyable album.

R30: 30th Anniversary World Tour

Personnel:
Alex Lifeson: guitars, vocals
Geddy Lee: vocals, bass guitar
Neil Peart: drums
Released: 22 November 2005
Label: Sanctuary Records
Recorded at Festhalle Frankfurt (Frankfurt am Main) on 24 September 2004
Mixed by Richard Chycki and Alex Lifeson
All music composed by Lee and Lifeson, with lyrics by Peart, except 'Der Trommler', music by Peart, 'Summertime Blues' by Cochran and Capeheart, and 'Crossroads' by Johnson
Chart positions: None (part of DVD package, not a separate release)

Lacking a new album of original material, Rush added tracks from *Feedback* to their set list, as if they needed to justify a tour. The promotional campaign, like the covers album, was put forward as a celebration of Rush's 30th anniversary. The *R30 Tour* ran from the end of May to the beginning of October 2004, concentrating mainly on North America, with two shows in Canada and three weeks in Europe.

This was the band's first visit to the United Kingdom in over 12 years, and they received a hero's welcome. The show in the Festhalle, Frankfurt, Germany, on 24 September was recorded and then released in both DVD and CD formats, although the double CD was only available as part of the DVD package.

Disc 1

'R30 Overture' (6.42)
An intriguing medley of excerpts from six songs, one from each of the first six albums, played in chronological order, shoots us through the 1970s with the main riffs of 'Finding My Way' (0.08 – 1.13), 'Anthem' (1.14 – 2.47), 'Bastille Day' (2.48 – 3.34), 'A Passage To Bangkok' (3.35 – 4.46), 'Cygnus X-1' (4.47 – 5.58) and 'Hemisphere's Prelude' (5.59 – 6.42).

'The Spirit Of Radio' (5.05)
'Force Ten' (4.10)
'Animate' (5.50)
'Subdivisions' (6.09)
'Earthshine' (5.42)
'Red Barchetta' (6.50)
'Roll The Bones' (6.22)
'The Seeker' (3.28)
'Tom Sawyer' (5.00)
'Dreamline' (5.20)

Disc 2
'Between The Wheels' (6.17)
'Mystic Rhythms' (5.23)

'Der Trommler' (9.02)
Initially, over a steady 4/4 pulse, Peart once again demonstrates how inventive and interesting 'Der Trommler' ('The Drummer') can be. A mid-section pause leads into a much more energetic display of Peart's virtuosity before side-stepping into more creativity over a tambourine beat in 3/4. Some impressive drum rolls lead into another high-energy workout for the man who once described his job as 'just hitting things with sticks'. A mixture of electronic percussion and acoustic drums brings this colourful masterclass to a close with a sequenced big-band blowout ('One O'Clock Jump'), all finished off with a gong.

'Resist' (4.33)
This is a re-run of the quite beautiful acoustic reinterpretation from *Rush In Rio*.

'Heart Full Of Soul' (2.45)
Interestingly, the *Feedback* version of this Yardbirds song also gets the twin acoustic guitar treatment. Peart returns in time for the second chorus.

'2112' (8.24)
Bizarrely, the second half of the second chorus of 'The Temples of Syrinx' has Lee adopting a pirate's accent and changing the words: 'The gifts of life are found down below'. Such a scamp! Such sacrilege! The band then segue straight into a storming 'Grand Finale', and a thunderous close, the sustained power chord of which becomes the introduction to ...

'Xanadu' (6.44)
... with the band picking the track up from the iconic, rotating ostinato, the power chords blasting into the concert hall. The band shorten the song, omitting the reprise of the initial instrumental, moving straight into the agonised-sounding final vocal section and supremely expressive solo. Power chords cut short the anticipated ending, leading straight into ...

'Working Man' (6.14)
An unexpected diversion into a reggae-based backing, with some dubious, regional vocal impersonations for the third verse, is soon dispensed with amidst the mother of all big rock endings.

'Summertime Blues' (3.41)
'Crossroads' (3.13)
'Limelight' (4.58)

Snakes And Arrows (2007)

Personnel:
Alex Lifeson: electric and acoustic guitars, mandola, mandolin, bouzouki
Geddy Lee: vocals, bass guitar, bass pedals, Mellotron
Neil Peart: drums, cymbals, electronic percussion, tambourine
Additional Musician:
Ben Mink: strings on 'Faithless'
Recorded at Allaire Studios, Woodstock, New York, and Grandmaster Recorders, Hollywood, California, between November and December 2006
Produced by Nick Rasulinecz and Rush
Released: 1 May 2007
Label: Atlantic Records
Chart positions: Canada: 3, US: 2, UK: 21
All music composed by Lee & Lifeson, with lyrics by Peart, except 'Hope' by Lifeson

Work on the next studio album began in January 2006. Lee and Lifeson came up with ideas at their home studios in Toronto, using a 'click track' as a guide drum part. Peart wrote at his new home in California, collaborating with his bandmates online, and travelling to Toronto and New York throughout the writing and recording phases.

The drummer arrived at the album title by accident whilst writing the lyrics to 'Armor And Sword'. He noted the Indian board game Leela, an early version of Snakes and Ladders, seeing the title as a description of the belief systems a child inherits. A painting by the Hindu scholar Harish Johari, called *The Leela Of Self Knowledge*, was developed as part of the artwork by Peart, with Hugh Syme incorporating it into the sleeve layout. The CD booklet also includes individual images for each of the song lyrics, all designed by the pair. The back cover features another Syme design: a pair of elderly hands clasp both a snake and an arrow. The trio are represented by a small green-sepia photo of the band, looking suspiciously like a Police lineup.

The group sought out a new producer, choosing a 32-year-old producer from Tennessee, Nick Rasulinecz, who had worked with the Foo Fighters and Velvet Revolver. Raskulinecz was a fan of the band, having watched them as a teenager on the *Moving Pictures* tour. Work began in September, with Raskulinecz encouraging Rush to explore their own limits and to incorporate the complex rhythmic and melodic ideas that were a dominant feature of their 1970s output. The main recording sessions took place in November and December, with the mixing completed in four weeks. The band's 18th album of original material was completed ahead of schedule.

'Far Cry' (5.18)

The song opens with a terrifically heavy and heavily syncopated aural attack of guitar, bass and drums over a repeated mandola drone in 4/4 time. Twelve seconds in and the first evidence of Rush raiding their back catalogue is the brief appearance of the 'Lifeson Chord' of 'Hemispheres' fame. This is followed by a wonderful swaggering guitar riff, which rocks out over three bars of 4/4, a bar of 3/4 and four further bars of 4/4, a sequence which is then repeated. This subsequent underlying music (a sound which could have been lifted from *Vapor Trails* with a drone guitar and a melodic bass riff taking centre stage) for the descriptive opening couplet: 'Pariah dogs and wandering madmen, barking at strangers and speaking in tongues'.

The spectacular chorus is anthemic and powerful despite the regretful nature of the lyrics: 'It's a far cry from the world we thought we'd inherit. It's a far cry from the way we thought we'd share it'. The lyrical attitude and musical energy are sustained throughout the song.

'Far Cry' is a powerful, committed and melodic opener. It would have been even better if taken at a quicker tempo. The introduction is reprised after the second chorus, which leads into an instrumental full of sustained lines from multiple Lifesons. The introduction reappears as a coda section, the song suspended by the 'Hemispheres' chord at its close. For fretboard fans reading this, it's an F#7(sus4).

'Armor And Sword' (6.36)

The title refers to the interpretation of religious faith – whether used for 'good' as a form of protection or 'bad' as a weapon – with some evocative lines: 'Blood is drained of colour by the flashes of artillery light' and 'The battle flags are flown at the feet of a God unknown' being just two examples. The repeated refrain – 'no one gets to their heaven without a fight' – is particularly appropriate.

Musically, the track switches between epic heaviness, grandiose melodic passages and subtle acoustic sections. The time signatures similarly move from 4/4 for the heavy rock sections to 3/4 for the softer verses. It's a joy to hear Rush operating at the top of their game, the main criticism being that, again, the tempo lacks urgency.

At six and a half minutes, the song feels overlong and a touch predictable with its relentless pulse. When Lifeson wades in with another screaming solo, there is the sense of too much being thrown into the mix; the vocals are frequently double-tracked, and whilst the choir of Lees is largely absent, this is sonically a very 'busy' track.

'Workin' Them Angels' (4.47)

Peart overheard the title phrase in an exchange between an elderly, married couple and felt a connection with his own life. Consequently, the lyrics contain several personal reflections. Peart's memory hums 'at the heart of a factory town', strums 'at the heart of a moving picture', 'drums at the heart of an English winter' and beats at 'the heart of an African village'. The chorus sums up his worldview well: 'All my life I've been working them angels overtime. Riding and driving and living so close to the edge'.

This track is a fine example of the excellent recorded sound Raskulinecz achieved in the studio: a huge soundscape, spacious and yet overwhelmingly heavy at times. This is also another song which swings between time signatures 6/8 (in the strongly melodic verses) and 4/4 (for the industrially heavy choruses).

An interesting diversion, and another first for the band, if not for the genre of heavy rock as a whole, is the inclusion of a bouzouki solo as a major feature of the instrumental section (2.37 – 2.59), backed by some baritone 'ooh'-ing from Lee. Otherwise, the song is a routinely structured composition. The combination of stirring melodies and an impressive recorded sound lifts what might be a typical 'mid-side' track into something spectacular.

'The Larger Bowl' (4.07)

A brisker track with an intriguing mix of Lees and an arpeggiated acoustic guitar introduction gives this song a modern folk feel. Taking its title from the fifth chapter of Peart's first book, *The Masked Rider* (1996), 'The Larger Bowl' addresses the justice and injustice of life, neatly summarised in the chorus: 'Some are blessed and some are cursed, the Golden One or scarred from birth, while others only see the worst, such a lot of pain on the earth'.

The lyric follows the pantoum form, after which the composition is subtitled. In this style of writing, the second and fourth lines of the first verse become the first and third lines of the next verse. Consequently, the second and fourth lines of the second verse become the first and third lines of the subsequent verse, and so on. This style of writing is Malaysian in origin, and the title had been lodged in Peart's memory since he came up with it during a cycling tour he undertook in West Africa in 1988.

Although the track maintains its folksy style throughout, the sound heavies up, particularly for the chorus, and Lifeson adds a tastily distorted, bluesy solo as the main part of the instrumental. This is another track that, whilst being straightforward in structure, benefits from wide-ranging changes in texture and dynamics combined with an incessantly catchy vocal melody to lift it well above the ordinary.

'Spindrift' (5.24)

Snakes And Arrows steps up a significant gear with its fifth track. 'Spindrift' is just fantastic. Here, Peart, always interested in natural phenomena, links the look and feel of a spindrift with turmoil within relationships, as well as a broader aspect of the geopolitical power struggles between the West and the East. His lyrics are superb: 'As the waves crash in on the western shore, it makes me feel uneasy. The spray that's torn away is an image for the way I feel'.

The first 30 seconds are eerily unsettling, with some backwards guitar and plenty of reverberation. A dissonant guitar arpeggio emerges from the sonic murk, a wondrous, strident riff takes hold and we're off. Bass and drums join in with Lee in a superb, high voice. The chorus ('What am I supposed to say?

Where are the words to answer you? When you talk that way?') is backed by a rising chromatic grind before falling back, perfectly reflecting the struggle of achieving resolution in a conflict.

At 2.43, the assault backs off somewhat with a softer yet still driving section and a wistful mix of melody and lyric ('A little closer to you, where is the wave that will carry me, a little closer to you?'). This leads into an understated guitar solo before the dial is turned back up for repeats of the chorus, the sound becoming stronger until another lapse back into the gentler refrain.

The play-out section adds a howling guitar melody above the all-conquering riff as this masterpiece goes into a too-quick fade, with Peart punishing his drums. The song actually ends before the fade is finished with a heavily reverberated effect.

'The Main Monkey Business' (6.01)

What is 'The Main Monkey Business'? Apparently, it is a phrase used by Geddy's mother to describe the philandering ways of a relative within the family! The first of the album's three – yes, three – instrumentals is the best of the bunch. 'The Main Monkey Business' is a complex, multi-faceted piece held together by an impressive groove and, for the most part, a constant, mid-paced tempo.

Whether it's the haunting Mellotron melody, the heavier section involving the occasional lurch into 7/4 time or one of Lifeson's greatest ever riffs (0.51), this is the band's best instrumental since 'YYZ'. The guitarist also turns in a beautiful, creamy solo at 2.50 and a dramatic concluding section that piles on the heaviness. Lee and Peart aren't sitting back and letting him have all the fun; their individual contributions are equally impressive.

The final section is surely one of the rockiest in the entire Rush canon. The drums sound like gunfire, the bass is pile-driving and the syncopated guitar chords build into a hugely impressive ending, which is rounded off, as the composition began, with a pretty descending chord sequence on the 12-string acoustic guitar.

'The Way The Wind Blows' (6.28)

The opening drum salvoes echo a battlefield, with tom-toms and snare playing a duet that grows in intensity and volume until, at 22 seconds in, Rush go right back to ... *Rush*. For the first time in a very long time (*Feedback* being an honourable exception), the band return to the blues rock of their debut album. Lifeson clearly relishes the opportunity to throw in some soulful, pained, bluesy bends in his solo section. It's an unexpected diversion, which makes a swift left-hand turn into another killer guitar riff, this one sounding like it's been inspired by 1970s Welsh heavy rock trio Budgie.

The lyrics savage organised religion; from the Middle East to the Middle West, it's 'like the Dark Ages', 'a world of superstition' where 'wide-eyed armies of the faithful pray, and pass the ammunition'. Peart doesn't hold back:

'It's a plague that resists all science' and they 'leave no child behind'. The chorus reflects upon how such ideas can influence us from childhood ('we can only grow the way the wind blows') and how we must adapt to each new situation (or be 'broken down blow by blow').

The musical backdrop to this onslaught switches between heavy, rocking passages and gentle, beautiful, acoustic-driven sections, all in 3/4. The blues makes a return (4.08 – 4.32) with Lifeson wrenching all manner of pain out of his gorgeous-sounding guitar, the music twisting again at 4.33 and introducing Eastern-style scales; a neat contrast with the broad-brush Western blues genre, and the more intricate harmonies of the music on the other side of the world.

This outstanding track closes with repeats of the chorus and Lee self-harmonising. The combination of intense lyrics and a wide panorama of different moods and styles marks 'The Way The Wind Blows' as another superb display of the myriad talents within the band, brought to astonishing sonic clarity and impact by Raskulinecz.

'Hope' (2.03)

A pretty enough interlude, or an acoustic-based noodling waste of time, depending upon your mood, this is a solo 12-string guitar instrumental played in D-A-D-A-A-D tuning by Lifeson. Similar in style to pieces by English folk guitarists John Renbourn, Bert Jansch and Davy Graham, the recording is the first take, which was mixed immediately afterwards.

'Faithless' (5.31)

The introduction to 'Faithless' carries vague echoes of *Vapor Trails* before opening out into a steadily paced verse. Here, Peart takes a more personal and defiant stance against the 'preaching voices', the 'empty vessels' that 'ring so loud'. The lyricist, with 'his own moral compass to steer by', doesn't 'have faith in faith' but 'believes in love', and 'that's faith enough' for him. 'Faithless' is another hymn to individualism, and the personal freedom that comes from making one's own decisions.

Another song to blend 3/4 and 4/4 time signatures, the arrangements and performances are immediately identifiable as Rush; the pulsing guitar, the prominent bass, the emotive vocals and the energetic and inventive drumming all add up to a whole that is much greater than the sum of its parts.

Lifeson is front and centre with another brooding beast of a solo, initially restrained but building in angst and complexity towards its close. This is another example of a guitarist in complete technical control of his instrument, yet making it sound alive, fresh and vital.

The chorus is the song's standout feature; a proud, uplifting and powerful section of music where the lyricist's stance is, once again, perfectly matched by the music of his colleagues. This brilliant track ends with a squall of feedback, fading away.

'Bravest Face' (5.12)

'Bravest Face' opens in powerful style with a rolling overdriven guitar figure, bass and drum stabs and an opening line: 'Though we might have precious little, it's still precious'. However, 17 seconds in, the track takes another unexpected twist. This time, we're into modern folk territory again, as a strummed acoustic guitar is the only accompaniment, with Lee indulging an individual quirk of his unique singing style, this being the occasional push into falsetto.

The lyrics focus on the disparity of life as portrayed by the media (television shows with upbeat themes, positive songs and stories with happy endings) paint optimistic pictures for us, but it's not an objective reality. Inevitably, Peart comes down hard on the side of what is real, really coming into his own with the choruses: 'In the sweetest child there's a vicious streak. In the strongest man there's a child so weak'. Our role in this world is to 'rise, and put on our 'bravest face''. We should make good use of our time and not waste it on trivialities, no matter how reassuring they may be.

Matching the words, the music builds dramatically for the chorus, building to a crescendo before abruptly reverting to the laid-back acoustic strumming. Rather than lazily repeating the contrasts of the first chorus, Peart presents a fresh set of contradictions: 'In the softest voice there's an acid tongue, in the oldest eyes there's a soul so young. In the shakiest will there's a core of steel. On the smoothest ride there's a squeaky wheel'. An idle writer would have been content with mere repetition; Peart has more comparisons to make, and he isn't going to hold his descriptive powers back.

By this point in the track, we might reasonably expect one of Lifeson's idiosyncratic fret burning outings, but here, he plays a relatively clean-sounding, blues-influenced solo, which continues under the repeated choruses played out over the light-touch acoustic backing. The power returns for a further chorus, full of fire and passion, which makes 'Bravest Face' another fine contribution to this very strong and consistently satisfying album.

'Good News First' (4.51)

Another heavy introduction propelled by vigorous overdriven guitar suddenly breaks down 42 seconds into a relatively quieter section, where Lee's studio-treated vocals sound laconically alien against the mixture of funky fills and scything, distorted power chords.

Reaching back into the mists of Rush's history, Peart revisits the writing of Ayn Rand, and her premise (the existence of a benevolent universe) is challenged. Again, the lyricist doesn't restrain himself, asking what happened to it. In the chorus, he addresses the enduring nature of beauty with some of his most romantic lines: 'You used to feel that way, the saddest words you would ever say. But I know you'll remember that day, and the most beautiful words I could ever say'.

Heavily distorted guitars, pounding bass and aggressive drums lift the energy to appropriate levels before falling back into the half-time groove of the second verse. Whilst the words are, at face value, addressing a struggle within a relationship, Peart opens up the debate to a far wider group of people, and this is a companion lyric to that presented on 'Bravest Face'; whatever the situation, one has to make the best of it, so give us 'the good news first'.

Despite the heavy rocking attitude and passionate commitment of the performances, 'Good News First' is the first track on the album to feel like an underachievement. The presence of another acoustic, almost poppy section starting at 3.02 ('Some would say they never fear a thing ... so do me that favour and tell me the good news first') adds some interest and contrast with what has gone before. However, the subsequent guitar solo sounds perfunctory, a marker at the end of a session that was left in place, deemed to be 'good enough'. Repeated powerful choruses bring this merely average song to a close.

'Malignant Narcissism' (2.17)

This mid-tempo instrumental is a distorted guitar, frenetic bass and intensive drum workout that gives each player room to shine within its limited lifespan. Relentlessly heavy, there is a slight lessening of the tension at 1.08, where, amidst a squall of feedback, some dialogue from the 2004 comedy film *Team America: World Peace* appears. The writers, Trey Parker and Matt Stone, were fans of the band and were happy for this to be included. A female voice is heard saying, 'Usually a case of malignant narcissism is brought on during childhood.'

'We Hold On' (4.13)

Another anthem to the stoic approach to life, 'We Hold On' focuses on problems within relationships, and the temptations to 'cut and run' when the going gets rough. The verses address the 'little battles' and 'stormy evenings' and the options of calling it 'quits', of driving 'away into the setting sun'. The chorus plays the longer game: 'Keep going until dawn. How many times must another line be drawn? We could be down and gone, but we hold on'.

Whilst this is all very worthy and well-worded, the accompanying music is less impressive. 'We Hold On' mixes quieter, chugging verses with a more full-blown and louder chorus. Lifeson employs some interesting, Eastern-based harmonies in his fills and solo section (2.30 – 3.01), but overall, this isn't the rousing final rocker that the album needed to maintain its high level of quality. After a third verse and chorus, and a furious-sounding instrumental play-out, rather than a fade, the track comes to a solid rock ending. 'We Hold On' is by no means a bad song; it just doesn't work as well or feel as inspired as the better tracks on the album.

Snakes & Arrows – Live (2008)

Personnel:
Alex Lifeson: electric and acoustic guitars, bass pedal synth
Geddy Lee: bass, synthesisers, vocals
Neil Peart: drums, percussion
Recorded at Rotterdam Ahoy, Rotterdam, The Netherlands, between 16 and 17 October 2007
Recorded by Francois Lamoureux
Mixed by Richard Chycki and Alex Lifeson
Released: 14 April 2008
Label: Atlantic Records
Chart positions: Canada: 8, US: 18, UK: 70
All music composed by Lee and Lifeson, with lyrics by Peart, except 'De Slagwerker', music by Peart; 'Hope', music by Lifeson

Snakes & Arrows – Live is another salvo of double CD and double DVD offerings. It was recorded during two performances of the first leg of the *Snakes And Arrows Tour* at the Ahoy Arena in Rotterdam, Holland, on 16 and 17 October 2007. The DVD features some additional material from the second leg of the tour, recorded at the Verizon Wireless Amphitheatre in Alpharetta, Georgia, Atlanta, on 22 July 2008. The 'DVD only' tracks are 'Ghost Of A Chance', 'Red Barchetta', 'The Trees' and '2112' ('Overture'/'The Temples Of Syrinx').

Disc 1

'Limelight' (4.48)

'Digital Man' (6.57)
YES! Finally!! This is a revelation!!! Shorn of its studio synth-pop trappings, 'Digital Man' is now an absolute stormer of a song: mighty, brooding and unstoppable. The 'poppier' sections of the song sound aggressive thanks to Lifeson's savage, distorted chords; the instrumental is now atmospheric and menacing and the guitar solo is full of angst and pain. The coda section becomes magnificent in this new interpretation. Brutal and unrelenting, Peart pounds his kit into near submission, Lee solos under Lifeson's rhythmic attack and the whole song is magically transformed into greatness. At last!

'Entre Nous' (5.18)
This is the first and only time this song appeared on a Rush live album.

'Mission' (5.39)
'Freewill' (6.02)
'The Main Monkey Business' (6.06)

'The Larger Bowl' (4.21)
'Secret Touch' (7.45)

'Circumstances' (3.47)
Another 'first live sighting' with this gem of a track.

'Between The Wheels' (6.01)
'Dreamline' (5.16)
'Far Cry' (5.20)
'Workin' Them Angels' (4.49)
'Armor And Sword' (6.57)

Disc 2
'Spindrift' (5.45)
'The Way The Wind Blows' (6.24)
'Subdivisions' (5.43)
'Natural Science' (8.34)
'Witch Hunt' (4.49)

'Malignant Narcissism'/'De Slagwerker' (10.42)
This short-but-sweet instrumental segues into 'De Slagwerker', the title being Dutch for The Drummer, and not, as has been suggested, a local prostitute. This is another unique display of extreme ability with plenty of audience approval. Peart's composition changes halfway through into a section involving electronic percussion. This mutates into what sounds like a soothing 'spa-music' section before an explosive 'Big Band' sequenced ending ('Cotton Tail' by Duke Ellington), which blows any remaining cobwebs away.

'Hope' (2.21)
Just a man, a 12-string acoustic guitar and an attentive audience of thousands listening to this pretty, folk-inspired composition, 'Hope' is a small oasis of melodic peace and tranquillity.

'Distant Early Warning' (4.54)
'The Spirit Of Radio' (5.03)

'Tom Sawyer' (5.48)
This is amusingly introduced by a South Park cartoon where the characters pretend to be Rush.

'One Little Victory' (5.27)
'A Passage To Bangkok' (3.57)
'YYZ' (5.17)

Time Machine 2011 – Live In Cleveland (2011)

Personnel:
Alex Lifeson: electric and acoustic guitars
Geddy Lee: vocals, bass guitar, keyboards
Neil Peart: drums, percussion
Recorded at Quicken Loans Arena, Cleveland, Ohio, on 15 April 2011
Mixed by Richard Chycki
Released: 8 November 2011
Label: Roadrunner Records
Chart positions: Canada: 59, US: 54, UK: 70
All music composed by Lee and Lifeson, with lyrics by Peart, except 'Moto Perpetuo', music by Peart; 'O'Malley's Break', music by Lifeson

A pointless live compilation, for this fan at least, was the appearance of *Working Men*, another CD/DVD package on 13 November 2009. This was a collection of previously released live recordings (with one fresh exception) taken from the band's tours of the first decade of the new century. It felt like a rip-off, but for fans new to the band and their prodigious output, it may well have worked in enticing extra members into the fold.

The tracks featured are 'Limelight', 'Freewill', 'Far Cry' and 'Tom Sawyer' from *Snakes & Arrows – Live*; 'The Spirit Of Radio', 'Dreamline', 'Subdivisions' and 'Working Man' from *R30*; and '2112'/'The Temples Of Syrinx', 'Closer To The Heart' and 'YYZ' from *Rush In Rio*. A previously unreleased version of 'One Little Victory' was included, possibly as aural catnip for the completist. I passed on this – the only Rush album not in my collection – until *R50* in 2025, that is.

Taking an 18-month break after the *Snakes And Arrows* tour, the band then convened in Los Angeles with plans to write a new album and undertake another tour. Two new songs, 'Caravan' and 'BU2B', recorded in April 2010, were released as a single on 1 June 2010, and were both featured on the *Time Machine* tour. Writing for the new album continued, with recording commencing after the end of the second leg of the tour in July 2011.

On 25 June 2010, Rush received a star on the Hollywood Walk of Fame in front of the Musicians Institute on Hollywood Boulevard. Alex and Geddy attended. Neil, shunning the limelight as was his want, was riding his motorcycle to the band's first date of the *Time Machine* tour, which commenced at the Hard Rock casino pavilion in Albuquerque four days later.

The tour was in two halves: July to October 2010, and then April to July 2011. It was the only occasion that *Moving Pictures* was played from start to finish live. The album was recorded at Quicken Loans Arena, Cleveland, Ohio, on 15 April 2011, and was once again issued as a CD and DVD package.

Disc 1
'The Spirit Of Radio' (5.02)
'Time Stand Still' (5.17)
'Presto' (6.33)

'Stick It Out' (4.22)
'Workin' Them Angels' (4.44)
'Leave That Thing Alone' (5.14)
'Faithless' (5.57)

'BU2B' (4.24)
Relentlessly and overwhelmingly heavy, 'BU2B' is the musical equivalent of being flattened by a tank, giving the fans an early display of the brilliance of the forthcoming *Clockwork Angels*.

'Freewill' (5.29)
'Marathon' (6.29)
'Subdivisions' (5.30)

'Tom Sawyer' (4.53)
So it begins: the first back-to-back, sequenced playing of *Moving Pictures*.

'Red Barchetta' (6.55)
After Lifeson's post-solo riff, we hear the bizarre sound of a pre-recorded Lee saying, 'No more for me, thanks. I'm driving'.

'YYZ' (4.33)

'Limelight' (4.32)
Commencing with fairground organ, spoken words, a bicycle bell, a whistle, a bus bell, and a brief excerpt from 'Battlescar' (the 'duet' song with Max Webster on that band's final studio album *Universal Juveniles*, released in 1980), this timeless classic finally starts to roll down familiar tracks.

Disc 2
'The Camera Eye' (10.10)
At the second and final climax ('The focus is sharp in the city' (London), Geddy adds a loud 'Yeah baby'. This is then immediately followed by a recording of actor Mike Myers repeating the same phrase in his 'Austin Powers' persona, and we then hear 'Bring out yer dead' voiced by Eric Idle, taken from the 1974 film *Monty Python And The Holy Grail*. Funny? Yes. Strange and inappropriate? Also Yes. But the crowd don't seem bothered at all by the taking of such liberties.

'Witch Hunt' (4.42)

'Vital Signs' (5.28)
As the final chord dies away, and to acknowledge the end of this part of the programme, Geddy says, 'It's hard to believe that's almost 31 years old. Almost as old as Lerxst over there.'

'Caravan' (5.37)
From the fairly old to the brand new, and with absolutely no diminution of quality, the sinister opening breaks out into some monster riffage, and it's incredible just how heavy this song is.

'Moto Perpetuo' (8.23)
Peart could never be accused of playing the same solo on every tour. The title is appropriate, being Latin for a composition that frequently changes and has a fast tempo. Here's another seemingly effortless (although obviously not effortless) display of the man's skill and musicality. There are some pleasing, sustained synth chords behind his formidable virtuosity, which, after the sound effect of a train, move into a 3/4 pulse with more supporting synth and a lighter, more percussive section. Some African influences then appear with more melodic keyboard washes before a brief pause and the final straight: the 'Big Band' ending ('Love For Sale' by Duke Ellington), proving that 'The Professor' is just at home in this very different genre as his prog rock roots.

'O'Malley's Break' (1.34)
In the Pre-Concert comedy video that opens the DVD, Peart portrays a stereotypical New York Irish-American cop, 'O'Malley', in an extended sketch set in a diner. The title of this instrumental is another nod towards the drummer taking a well-earned, if brief, rest.

'O'Malley's Break' is just Lifeson, his 12-string guitar, and another beautiful composition written specifically for this tour. It's a delightful contrast, and is another 'out-of-genre' display of tasteful playing that merges seamlessly into the introduction for ...

'Closer To The Heart' (3.28)
The final verse and refrain are played out over a shuffle rhythm that Status Quo would be proud of. This abnormality is soon dispensed with, and the band revert to a punchy 4/4 rhythm to close.

'2112' (7.10)
'Far Cry' (6.23)

'La Villa Strangiato' (7.40)
The first of the encores, 'La Villa Strangiato' begins in a most bizarre fashion with a drum rhythm, some happy-sounding keyboards and an accordion, developing a German 'Oompah Band' sound. What, exactly, is going on here? Then, the universe rights itself as the band blast into the main first theme.

'Working Man' (6.41)
... another musical side step. A reggae rhythm establishes itself (the band are clearly having a lot of fun by now) and, as this is Cleveland, the song

can only be 'Working Man', can't it? Once the vocals start, we know what's going on, and just prior to the second chorus, the band blast back into full rock mode.

'Working Man' receives the biggest of slowed-down, big-rock endings, with a brief excerpt from the 'Cygnus X-1' main riff, leaving the crowd ecstatic, as Lee declares them 'the best audience – ever.'

Clockwork Angels (2012)

Personnel:
Alex Lifeson: guitars, keyboards
Geddy Lee: vocals, bass guitar, keyboards, bass pedals
Neil Peart: drums, cymbals, tambourine
Additional musicians
Jason Sniderman: piano ('The Garden')
Strings arranged and conducted by David Campbell, and recorded at Ocean Way Studios, Los Angeles, California
Recorded at Blackbird Studios, Nashville, and Revolution Recordings, Toronto, in April 2010 and between October and December 2011
Recorded by Richard Chycki
Mixed by Nick Rasulinecz at Henson Studios, Los Angeles, California
Produced by Nick Rasulinecz and Rush
Released: 8 June 2012
Label: Roadrunner Records
Chart positions: Canada: 1, US: 2, UK: 21
All music composed by Lee and Lifeson, with lyrics by Peart

Further recognition of the band's achievements came in May 2012 when they received the Governor General's Performing Arts Award for Lifetime Artistic Achievement at Rideau Hall in Ottawa. This was followed in 2013 by the band being commemorated with their own Canadian postage stamp featuring the Starman of *2112* fame.

For their final (as it turned out) studio album, Rush, once again never content to stand still and repeat themselves, decided that their next record should be in a form they had never previously explored; that of the full-length concept album. Whilst much of their 1970s output had featured long songs ('By-Tor And The Snow Dog' (*Fly By Night*), 'The Necromancer' (*Caress Of Steel*), 'Xanadu' and 'Cygnus X-1'(*A Farewell To Kings*), and 'La Villa Strangiato' (*Hemispheres*), and extending to 'whole side epics with '2112' (*2112*) and 'The Fountain Of Lamneth' (*Caress Of Steel*), the band had never released an album telling only one story. The challenge and the enthusiasm for the project would propel them to one of several career peaks.

In an interview with *Classic Rock* in December 2018, Geddy said:

> Ever since we came back after Neil's terrible tragedy with his family and having had those five dark years we were away, every tour I did with Rush I savoured. I would say that period from coming back after Neil's tragedy to the very end was the golden years for me. I felt like I appreciated every gig, every note that we played. The camaraderie that the three of us had, I never took it for granted, not one day. So I would say that was my happiest time in Rush.

Setting the tale in a 'steampunk' future (a world reliant on steam and chemicals, rather than electronics) was an interesting choice, transporting the listener into an alien, and yet oddly familiar environment. Another break from 'the norm' was the inclusion of a string section on several tracks. *Clockwork Angels* was also their longest release, clocking in at over 66 minutes.

The cover artwork is stunning. A red, black and white image of a clock face marked with alchemic symbols, the hands frozen at just before quarter past nine (21.12), floats in front of cyclonic clouds. The sumptuous hardback CD booklet features the song lyrics, plus some narrative text to help guide the listener through the story, together with some stunning images by Hugh Syme to further reinforce the world and circumstance of the tale. This is reproduced in the song reviews below.

In *Time Stand Still*, the 2016 DVD of the final tour, Neil reflected on *Clockwork Angels*:

> I think that this is the album we always wanted to make since we first got together. The layers of the drumming on there, the music we created, working with a string section was something that we always talked about doing, the size of the story and the resolution of the story. That tour and that album totally pleased me, and I've never had that before. It was a huge accomplishment for us.

Clockwork Angels is dedicated to the band's long-term photographer, Andrew MacNaughtan, who died on 24 January 2012. All the quotes in these sections are taken from Peart's liner notes for the album.

'Caravan' (5.40)

> It seems a lifetime ago, which, of course, it was, all that and more. For a boy, life on the farm was idyllic, but for the young man I became, that very peace and predictability were stifling, unbearable. I had big dreams, and needed a big place to explore them, the whole wide world. Near our village of Barrel Arbor, the steam-liners touched down and travelled on rails along the Winding Pinion River toward Crown City. Watching them pass in the night, how I prayed to get away...

'Caravan' has an autobiographical feel. Peart's father ran a farm machinery dealership, where Neil would work when old enough to supplement his income from as many gigs as he could play. We hear the inner voice of the youngster who longs to leave his home and explore the world again, drawing parallels with Peart's own life, a point emphasised in the song's refrain: 'I can't stop thinking big'.

The young Peart had dreamt of becoming a professional drummer, constantly playing in local bands, and even moving to London to try his luck without success. A move back to Canada and a preparedness to keep drumming meant that the vacant drum stool following original Rush drummer John Rutsey's departure gave him the opportunity he craved.

Opening with atmospheric train bells and hydraulic engines, the central riff appears in isolated fragments on keyboards, with a string section and hi-hat immediately adding tension. Thirty-eight seconds in, the riff blasts through on guitar, and what stands out immediately is just how heavy this song, and so much of the album, is. The music pulses with energy and power, the strings adding much to the overall effect, matched by Lee's wailing vocal delivery.

A funky instrumental section after the second chorus (3.22) is followed by the first in a series of absolute monster riffs on the album. A squealing guitar solo underlines the enthusiasm and power to great effect before the song returns to repeated refrains, bringing it to a tight end.

'BU2B' (5.10)

> We were always taught that we lived in 'the best of all possible worlds'. The Watchmaker ruled from Crown City through the Regulators; the alchemist-priests gave us coldfire for power and light, and everything was well ordered. We accepted our various individual fates as inevitable, for we had also been taught, 'Whatever happens to us must be what we deserve, for it could not happen to us if we did not deserve it.'

There is a throwback to the authoritarian priests of 'The Temples Of Syrinx' with the lyrics to 'Brought Up To Believe', an unwieldy title that was shortened to an acronym during recording, which subsequently stuck. Here, however, the story's ruler is a Watchmaker who 'loves us all to death'. The lyrics address questions of predestination and free will. Should we accept whatever religious, cultural and ethnic traditions we are born into and are surrounded by as children? Or should we reject such teachings in search of our own solutions?

A haunting introduction of acoustic guitar, delay and ghostly vocals accompanies the first verse, which is soon crushed under the monumental weight of the second of the album's killer riffs. The first verse is repeated over this, with a second verse continuing the criticism of organised religion: 'The universe has a plan, all is for the best, some will be rewarded, and the Devil will take the rest'.

The music moves into double-time for the urgent-sounding chorus, underpinned by a discordant guitar drone, cutting out completely, leaving Lee's vocal of the word 'death' completely exposed, and all the more effective for it. Another pair of vitriolic verses and a further driving chorus (just marvel at the degree of heavy rocking on display here) leads into a repeated new section with some classic Lifeson arpeggios underneath 'Until our final breath, the joy and pain that we receive must be what we deserve. I was brought up to believe'. A howling guitar solo among all the sonic mayhem cuts through before the final choruses and an abrupt end to this almost overwhelming song.

'Clockwork Angels' (7.31)

> The place I had most wanted to see – Chronos Square, at the heart of Crown City. I had seen many images of the city before, and Chronos Square, but nothing could convey its immensity – the heaven-reaching towers of the Cathedral of the Timekeepers, or the radiant glory of the Angels – Land, Sea, Sky and Light – bathed in the brilliant glow of the floating globes.

The title track, the longest on the album, is a sprawling, multi-faceted work. Another dream-like introduction with Oriental overtones gradually builds into a pulsating groove where a wall of guitars is joined by the pulverising percussionist, the mood suddenly lightening at 1.08, where the vocals burst through with surprising clarity. The vocals describe the effect the 'Clockwork Angels' have on the city's people, rather than directly describing the entities. Against another heavy backdrop, the Angels 'promise every treasure to the foolish and the wise, Goddesses of mystery, spirits in disguise, every pleasure we bow and close our eyes, clockwork angels promise every prize'. This suggests a throwback to the priests of 'The Temples Of Syrinx' ('2112'): 'All the gifts of life are held within these walls'. There is therefore no need to explore, question or seek to improve oneself; everything is provided for your worldly needs. The combination of words, thunderous drumming, the massive guitar sound and compelling vocals makes this an outstanding example of Rush at their very best.

Lifeson unleashes a squealing, idiosyncratic solo that climbs to a climax as the music turns a corner into an unexpected, slow, bluesy shuffle. This forms an unexpected backing to the next section, where a ghostly-sounding Lee sings words from the Book of Proverbs of the Old Testament – 'Lean not upon your own understanding' – continuing with 'ignorance is well and truly blessed. Trust in perfect love and perfect planning. Everything will turn out for the best'. This can be interpreted as a reaffirmation of the mantra of the Clockwork Angels and The Watchmaker.

The sound returns, as if from beyond the grave, for the final verse and repeated choruses. The song closes tantalisingly on the repeated 'As if to fly' before another power trio bludgeoning as the music ends with a hint of the Eastern style opening, and a whispered question, laden with reverb, from the voice of the Pedlar (actually spoken by Peart in the studio): 'What do you lack?'

'The Anarchist' (6.52)

> A foggy woodland road, a crowded village square, the busy streets of Crown City, a wandering pedlar travels the land, uttering the ageless call 'What do

> you lack?' Walking among the people, who are so content, so blind, the Anarchist hears the pedlar's call and sneers derisively. 'What do I lack? Ah ... vengeance?'

Given that, in Peart's steampunk universe, the Watchmaker can be seen as a benevolent God, is the Anarchist, therefore, the Devil? Or is it a metaphor for the philosophical conflict between order and chaos? Or that of conflicting political orthodoxies? Peart's imagined universe has several interpretations.

This makes the music for the fourth track a puzzling contribution to the story; it has echoes of the power-punk sound of Green Day in its drivingly melodic, major-key, up-tempo, rocking style. The titular character is malevolent, consumed by anger and bitterness from his life experiences, and seeking to strike against those who have not endured his suffering. The chorus sums him up best: 'The lenses inside of me that paint the world black, the pools of poison, the scarlet mist that spills over into rage'.

Putting the incongruous juxtaposition of lyrics and music aside, there are some terrific moments here; the unrelentingly rocking beat, the grinding guitar and the fabulous bass melody, which cuts through the melee, all sound like a band living their best lives. The interplay between bass and drums just before the lyrics begin is especially impressive.

The bridge section at 4.48, where the tempo drops into half time, is anthemic, developing into a short Lifeson solo, which brings to mind elements of Ritchie Blackmore's work on 'Stargazer' (from Rainbow's 1976 album *Rising*). A further chorus, and a reprise of some of the introduction, brings this epic number to a close, sound effects segueing neatly into the next song ...

'Carnies' (4.52)

> I found work with a travelling carnival, and for the Midsummer Festival in Crown City, our games and rides were set up right in the middle of the Square, beneath the Angels. One night, amid the noise and confusion of the crowded midway, I saw a man walking with wires and wooden barrels. He stood and turned – the Anarchist – holding a clockwork detonator in his hand. I called out to warn the crowd, then suddenly he threw the device at me, and I caught it automatically, just as the people turned to look my way.

... and Exhibit C in the series of monster riffs punches the listener straight between the ears. It almost references 'Working Man' in its ponderous, overwhelming sonic attack. Lee's voice rises up the octave to ride above the fury.

The music moves into double time for more evocative lyrics – 'A glint of iron wheels, bodies spin in a clockwork dance, the smell of flint and steel, a wheel of fate, a game of chance' – before a surreal, poppy chorus appears at 1.21.

The second section of lyrics, detailing the terrorists' bomb attack, returns to the titanic riff/double time section before yet another spectacular burst of Lifeson's rhythmic skills. This is intermingled with a melodic solo before the final verse details the attack. There is a return to the pop-style choruses, interspersed with more sonic destruction via reprises of the two main riffs. Rush have never sounded so overwhelmingly heavy.

'Halo Effect' (3.14)

> I had fallen helplessly in love with one of the performers. She was so different from 'the girl I left behind', and I was beginning to understand that I had only pretended she was right for me. I pursued my beautiful acrobat relentlessly until she let me be with her – then I suffered her rejection and contempt. Once again, I had created the idea of the perfect soul mate and tried to graft it onto her. It didn't fit. Such illusions have coloured my whole life.

And relax, for 'Halo Effect' gives the listener time to breathe as a beautiful acoustic guitar passage summons in Lee's soft voice in this regret-filled love song, which considers the idealistic images a new partner can project before reality inevitably reasserts itself. 'Halo Effect' soon becomes Rush's tasteful version of that much derided form, the power ballad, with its mixture of quiet and heavy sections, heightened by the evocative string section.

'Seven Cities Of Gold' (6.32)

> The legend had passed down for generations. Far across the Western Sky, where the steam-liners could not fly, lay a wilderness land hiding seven cities of gold. I dared the crossing on one of the stout ships that followed the trade route to Poseidon, a tough port city. I worked there for a while on the steam-liners that served the alchemy mines, then eventually set out into the Redrock Desert. The stories were sculpted into unearthly monuments, and the country grew cold as I travelled north in search of the most famous City of Gold, Cibola. Its name had sounded in my dreams since childhood.

The adventure resumes. The narrator, broken-hearted and alone, journeys ever onwards, accompanied by a furiously funky bass riff over which Lifeson lays down sounds of distorted torture against Peart's rock-solid rhythms. Out of this emerges yet another monster riff, and the song proper.

Inspired by the explorations of New Mexico, where fabled civilisations were believed to exist, but never discovered, 'Seven Cities Of Gold' is another heavyweight contribution to the tale. A catchy chorus and an instrumental section (4.02 – 4.50), where Lifeson unleashes all manner of feedback-laced pain, only adds to this superior composition, perfectly encapsulated by the wailing vocals and underpinned by a riff of monolithic proportions.

The track ends untidily, a mess of distortion, delay, reverb and sonic agony, as if to underline the final verse lyrics: 'That gleam in the distance could be heaven's gate, a long-awaited treasure at the end of my cruel fate ...'

'The Wreckers' (5.01)

> Narrowly escaping a frozen death in that desert, I made my way back to Poseidon and found a berth on a homeward ship. Caught in a terrible storm, we seemed to find salvation in an unexpected signal light. Steering toward it, we soon learned it was false – placed by the denizens to lure ships to their doom on the jagged reefs. They plundered the cargoes and abandoned the crews and passengers to the icy waves. I was the only survivor.

Another song where the upbeat, bouncy music is at odds with the darkly descriptive lyrics, 'The Wreckers' works despite this strange mixture. It opens with a chordal riff that has The Who tattooed all over it. The lyrics are based upon genuine acts of deception and destruction described in Daphne du Maurier's 1936 novel *Jamaica Inn*. The music and lyrics of 'The Wreckers' sound more aligned when it hits its chorus: 'All I know is that sometimes you have to be wary of a miracle too good to be true ... cause sometimes the target is you.'

Again, the appearance of the string section carries the music back towards more serious intent, sounding particularly ominous in the bridge section ('the breakers roar on an unseen shore, in the teeth of an icy grave, the human chain leaves a bloody stain, washed away in the pounding waves'). Luckily, by its close, the track has left behind its Who influences and sails into a fade, sounding fantastic.

'Headlong Flight' (7.20)

> Thinking back over my life and telling stories about my 'great adventures', they didn't always feel that grand at the time. But on balance, I wouldn't change anything. In the words of one of our great alchemists, Friedrich Gruber, 'I wish I could do it all again.'

'Headlong Flight' is the pièce de résistance: an acknowledgement of an illustrious history wrapped up in the sheen of an aggressive modern production. In the same way the tale's narrator recalls his many adventures, Rush pay tribute to their past with the best track of this album. The music was originally an instrumental with the title 'Take That Lampshade Off Yo Head!'

Opening with yet another stormer of a riff, this time played initially on the bass, guitar and drums add fire and fury before the ghost of the main riff of

'Bastille Day' (*Caress Of Steel*) rears its fabulous head at 43 seconds. A charged, melodic chorus ('some days were dark ... some nights were bright, I wish I could live it all again') is another high point.

The tempo drops down into half speed for a new, yet still heavy section where the protagonist reflects upon his life, concluding, 'Oh, how I wish I could live it all again'. This recurring refrain, a tacit nod to Freddie Gruber, who had expressed this very sentiment when discussing his long life, was a view to which Peart did not personally subscribe, even in this retrospective lyric.

The instrumental section (3.55 – 5.47) retains the frenetic pace with a surprising detour. After a spectacular section of drums and riffing, there is a homage to the instrumental section of 'By-Tor And The Snow-Dog' (*Fly By Night*), complete with an intense, wah-wah-based, screaming lead solo. The energy just doesn't let up, piling into another verse and a repeated section of choruses. As a celebration of the band's history and tenacity, 'Headlong Flight' delivers everything a fan could want.

'The Pedlar – 2'/'BU2B2' (1.28)

> The ever-wandering pedlar; 'What do you lack?' Those fateful words, 'What do you lack?', spark an inner monologue about all I have lost. No more boundless optimism, no more faith in greater powers, too much pain, too much grief and too much disillusion. Despite all that, I realise the great irony that although I now believe only in the exchange of love, even that little faith follows the childhood reflex that 'I was brought up to believe.'

The album's final tracks change the focus from the past to the here and now, with the narrator's thoughts, eloquently sung, backed by synthesiser and strings. Another lyric written in pantoum form, a green shoot of hope appears in the final section of words: 'I still choose to live and give, even when I grieve. Though the balance tilts against me I was brought up to believe'.

'Wish Them Well' (5.25)

> Victimised, bereaved and disappointed, seemingly at every turn, I still resist feeling defeated or cynical. I have come to believe that anger and grudges are burning embers in the heart, not worth carrying through life. The best response to those who wound me is to get away from them – and wish them well.

In the CD booklet, the image supporting this song's lyrics sums the track up best; a piece of parchment is on fire at its edges, the past being eliminated from the present in order to enhance the future. Peart opines that it is better for the individual to turn one's back on people or situations now irrelevant to the life you are currently living, and walk away. This is stressed as an act of maturity, not malice.

A straightforward, verging on brutal at times, rocker, 'Wish Them Well' encapsulates power and melody effectively, with the surprising inclusion of a high-pitched Lee singing right at the top of his range in the recurring echo of the song's title. Another mixture of a 'Who' like full-frontal assault with a melodic, arpeggio section (which throws in the occasional bar of 6/4 time amongst the relentless 4/4), the song is a high-powered hymn to the four wisdoms of the stoical approach to life: wisdom, courage, temperance and justice.

The track, whilst busy, is relatively straightforward in structure. Lifeson throws in another impressive, blues-influenced solo, which leads straight into another headbangers' delight of a riff. Repeated refrains rollick away into the fade of this celebratory anthem.

'The Garden' (6.59)

> Long ago, I read a story from another timeline about a character named Candide. He also survived a harrowing series of misadventures and tragedies, then settled on a farm near Constantinople. Listening to a philosophical rant, Candide replied, 'That is all very well, but now we must tend our garden.' I have now arrived at that point in my own story. There is a metaphorical garden in the acts and attitudes of a person's life, and the treasures of that garden are love and respect. I have come to realise that the gathering of love and respect – from others and for myself – has been the real quest in my life. 'Now we must tend our garden.'

'The Garden' has a symphonic sweep. From the high-pitched bass ostinato and sustained strings of the introduction, via the gently strummed acoustic guitar accompaniment of the first verses, to the chiming arpeggios and increasing texture of the chorus, 'The Garden' just keeps on growing.

The careful arrangement of instrumentation and changes in dynamics give this relatively uncomplicated composition its strength and character. At 3.37, there is a beautiful, atmospheric piano accompaniment to the most affecting lyrics: 'The future disappears into memory with only a moment between. Forever dwells in that moment, hope is what remains to be seen'.

The final guitar solo (and who were we to know that this would be the final studio song by the band) is moody, understated and utterly magnificent. Even more notable is the fact that it is the one Lifeson recorded as a demo.

Firing on all musical cylinders, this high-quality ballad cruises its way slowly to a final chord, and that's it – there is no more. 'The Garden' is another high point on a collection that delivers in every department throughout, and in retrospect, is a fine epitaph for the band, both musically and lyrically.

Clockwork Angels Tour (2013)

Personnel:
Alex Lifeson: guitar, vocals
Geddy Lee: vocals, bass
Neil Peart: drums
Recorded at US Airways Center, Phoenix, Arizona; American Airlines Center, Dallas, Texas; and AT&T Center, San Antonio, Texas, between 25 November and 30 November 2012
Mixed by Mike Fraser, with digital editing by Richard Chycki
Released: 19 November 2013
Label: Atlantic Records
Chart positions: Canada: 75, US: 33, UK:65
All music composed by Lee and Lifeson, with lyrics by Peart, except 'Here It Is!', 'Drumbastica' and 'The Percussor'/'Binary Love Theme'/'Steambanger's Ball', music by Peart; 'Peke's Repose', music by Lifeson

The *Clockwork Angels Tour* (Part 1) ran from September through to December 2012. On 18 April 2013, in the midst of a long break from the tour, the trio were inducted into the Rock 'n' Roll Hall of Fame at the Nokia Centre in Los Angeles. Not remotely phased by this long-overdue acceptance, the band commenced the second part of the tour five days later. More dates in America, England and some in Europe followed before the band finished up the tour in Canada, in Kansas City, on 4 August 2013.

Featuring songs recorded at three separate venues in late November 2012 (Dallas, Phoenix and San Antonio), and with 11 of the tracks featuring the *Clockwork Angels* String Ensemble, the live album of the tour pulls no punches. The look and sound of both the CD and the DVD are very impressive: the package features three hours of live music, three drum solos and over 30 songs.

Disc 1

'Subdivisions' (5.39)

'The Big Money' (6.02)
Just before the end, a pre-recorded Geddy intones 'One million dollars' to amusing effect.

'Force Ten' (5.35)
Lifeson's solo is very different to the original; here, he sounds agitated and incredibly creative – unleashed may be a better word for it.

'Grand Designs' (5.16)
'The Body Electric' (4.52)
'Territories' (6.47)

'The Analog Kid' (5.25)
'Bravado' (5.46)

'Where's My Thing?'/'Here It Is!' (8.23)
An impressive bass solo over a single sustained synth chord acts as an introduction to this groove-laden piece. Following the heavy proggy section mid-way through, Lee and Lifeson go for a brief Show-Biz Lie Down as the music segues into another fresh Peart composition, which, apart from the occasional paradiddle fill and the heavy snare-centric ending, is new to fans' ears. Despite having some synth sounds supplied by triggers, 'Here It Is!' sounds more like the traditional 'mid-gig' drum solos before Peart refined the genre. There is a brief reprise of the main theme of 'Where's My Thing?' to conclude this section.

'Far Cry' (5.36)

Disc 2
'Caravan' (5.42)
'Clockwork Angels' (8.13)
'The Anarchist' (7.00)
'Carnies' (5.16)
'The Wreckers' (5.28)

'Headlong Flight'/'Drumbastica' (8.17)
When the listener is expecting the extended instrumental section, the song suddenly breaks into 'Drumbastica', which is another monumental display of sheer power and technique. It features triggered sample 'stabs' of Lee and Lifeson's riffs from the song (4.29 – 5.30) before the duo reappear and launch into the 'By-Tor' tribute instrumental.

'Peke's Repose'/'Halo Effect' (5.15)
The title comes from one of the many inter-band nicknames; Peart was 'Peke', hence the title for his rest break. Lifeson was Leke, and Lee became Deke. 'Peke's Repose' is another beautiful solo composition for acoustic-sounding guitar by Lifeson. The sound and fury of what's gone before temporarily dissipates as he conjures up a beautiful, delicate instrumental with Celtic undertones, enhanced by the DADGAD tuning.

'Seven Cities Of Gold' (6.24)

'Wish Them Well' (6.41)
Between 5.20 and 5.34, there is some odd 'Dancing Dialogue' between Lee and Lifeson, which seems out of character for a song with an important lyrical message. Over a poppy, funk percussion groove, we hear:

Lee: This is where I try to get this man to dance. Come on, Lerxsty.
Lifeson: I'm dancing alright. I look like I've got something in my shoe.
Lee: That's not a dance.
Lifeson: Yeah, you look like you know how to dance, buddy!

The song then resumes its course into the final bars of the play-out and a sustained ending. Bizarre? Yes. Funny? Also Yes. But here? Not sure.

'The Garden' (7.16)

Disc 3
'Dreamline' (5.17)

'The Percussor'/'Binary Love Theme'/'Steambanger's Ball' (3.10)
Another new drum and percussion solo from Peart, this one features plenty of melodic triggered samples over a solid 4/4 pulse. The scene then shifts to African rhythms and tones, and then a Chinese mood, with more samples including plenty of sounds of 'found percussion' (corrugated metal, for example), and, erm, a steam train!

'Red Sector A' (5.21)
'YYZ' (4.52)
'The Spirit Of Radio' (6.28)
'Tom Sawyer' (5.57)
'2112' (8.24)

'Limelight' (4.43)
This is a sound-check recording and is a fascinating insight into a 'behind the scenes' run-through of the live performance, but without the presence of a crowd. The band are in rehearsal mode here, and on occasions, Lee dispenses with various lyrics or complete sections of vocals. The song ends with some funky messing about between the trio.

'Middletown Dreams' (5.23)
The final three songs are described as bonus tracks, although that description is a bit of a stretch for this number.

'The Pass' (5.05)
'Manhattan Project' (5.21)

R40 Live (2015)

Personnel
Alex Lifeson: guitar, vocals
Geddy Lee: vocals, bass
Neil Peart: drums
Recorded at Air Canada Centre, Toronto, Canada, on 17 and 19 June 2015
Recorded and mixed by David Bottril
Released: 20 November 2015
Label: Atlantic Records
Chart positions: Canada: 30, US: 24, UK: 47
All music composed by Lee and Lifeson, with lyrics by Peart, except 'The Story So Far', music by Peart

On 8 May 2015, Rush began what would be their final tour. In an interview with *Classic Rock* magazine in January 2025, Alex said:

> We were playing so well; the shows were so much fun for us and our audience, and we had good energy despite playing three-hour shows in our 60s. Ged and I were disappointed that Neil demanded playing only a limited number of dates, which precluded a UK and European run. I think a dozen or so more dates would have made us a bit more accepting. And then there was a point where I think Neil was open to maybe extending the run and adding in a few more shows, but then he got this painful infection in one of his feet. I mean, he could barely walk to the stage at one point. They got him a golf cart to drive him to the stage. And he played a three-hour show, with the intensity he played every single show. That was amazing, but I think that was the point where he decided that the tour was only going to go on until that final show in LA.

North America received the most attention, together with five dates in Canada, the *R40 Tour* closing a 30-date schedule at the Forum in Los Angeles on 1 August 2015.

This CD and DVD assault on Rush fans' senses is based on an intriguing concept. The band seemingly travel back through time, opening with songs from *Clockwork Angels* and finishing with a medley of tunes that predate Peart's arrival in 1974. Appropriately enough, the CD/DVD performance was recorded in the band's hometown, Toronto. As Philip Wilding described it in the accompanying CD booklet, the show opens with...

> ... a grand design; a state-of-the art stage that pivots, rolls and dives, and brings 'Clockwork Angels' into bombastic, colourful life before marching stridently back in time (through theatre stages, a panoply of band and fan shots, the accrued memories of a life spent playing live) to a mocked-up school gym and the band playing there; a solitary bass amp set on the chair

> behind Geddy Lee, a mirror ball spiralling crazily above, casting thin rods of light like a light rain across the crowd. 'Working Man' coming to a shuddering halt as the band's beginning becomes their end.

The back-through-time set list idea was not an album-by-album retrospective. No songs from *Test For Echo* featured, and the band jumped from 1991's *Roll The Bones* straight back to 1984's *Grace Under Pressure*. Songs from *Presto*, *Hold Your Fire* and *Power Windows* were ignored. These albums had, of course, been well represented on the previous *Clockwork Angels Tour* CD. It would have made for a more cohesive narrative if the concept had been strictly adhered to. It's not as if the band lacked decent material anywhere in their extensive canon of work.

Disc 1
'The World Is...The World Is' (2.10)
Not a new song, nor a mangling of 'Tom Sawyer', this is a pre-recorded, fast-forward-through-time medley featuring brief excerpts from many of the trio's most famous songs. It commences (after the groundswell synth of the start of 'Overture' from '2112' – 1976) with the opening riff of 'Finding My Way' (*Rush* – 1974), concluding with 'Working Them Angels' (*Snakes & Arrows* – 2007). Then, the band crash through the PA with the initial riff to 'The Anarchist'.

'The Anarchist' (7.07)
'Headlong Flight' (8.45)
'Far Cry' (5.31)
'The Main Monkey Business' (6.08)
'How It Is' (4.45)
'Animate' (6.15)
'Roll The Bones' (6.05)
'Between The Wheels' (5.58)

'Losing It' (5.55)
The synth era begins with a song never previously aired on a live album. Joined by Ben Mink (who played violin on the original recording), the dynamics and textural changes are fully realised. Mink's solo (to which some highly effective delay has been added) sounds even better than before. He sounds like – and, of course, is for this song – an integral part of the band, as the track builds to an aching climax and a final, sad chord.

'Subdivisions' (5.49)
Again? Not 'New World Man'? Not the rebooted and upgraded 'Digital Man'? I'd even give 'Chemistry' a free pass if it received a heavied-up treatment. No, this live staple is here again. It's not a case of familiarity breeding contempt, but *Signals* does have better songs on it. This is the final song of the first set.

Disc Two
'Tom Sawyer' (4.58)
'YYZ' (4.32)

'The Spirit Of Radio' (5.03)
Fortunately, Lee seems to have abandoned hopes of an alternative career as an impersonator by the time the reggae section appears.

'Natural Science' (8.32)
'Jacob's Ladder' (7.34)
'Hemisheres – Prelude' (4.19)

'Cygnus X-1'/'The Story So Far' (9.21)
...another surprise, and a very welcome 'blast from the past'. This 'Cygnus X-1' is the instrumental section of the original recording, starting with the iconic bass riff. Just before the vocal section, we are transported into 'The Story So Far', which is more Peart magnificence. Here, the focus is less on samples and more on pure drumming, supported by some triggered synth chords, many changes of dynamics and impressive displays of controlled brilliance. Given that this solo is an integral part of the 'Cygnus X-1' experience, the sound swings between the spooky and the intergalactic. A fantastic drum roll brings Lee and Lifeson back to the stage for a crushing version of the rest of the song, but played entirely as an instrumental. It is truly breathtaking stuff.

'Closer To The Heart' (3.08)
'Xanadu' (10.40)

'2112' (12.15)
No final tour would be complete without at least some of the band's first breakthrough album. Here, we have 'Overture', 'The Temples Of Syrinx', 'Presentation' (a welcome surprise) and 'Grand Finale'. Officially, this is the end of the gig. Except, of course, it isn't ...

Disc 3
'Mel's Rockpile' (1.36)
This is not a new piece of music; instead, we have a spoof introduction for the band in the early stages of their second incarnation. After a few seconds of some recorded jazz funk instrumental, we hear Eugene Levy, who gives the band a typical 'support band' introduction.

'Lakeside Park'/'Anthem' (5.29)

'What You're Doing'/'Working Man' (9.35)
There is an excerpt from the never officially released track 'Garden Road', which is a shuffle without vocals but with plenty of guitar. This short

instrumental extract may have confused some of the crowd, who hadn't purchased an unofficial live CD upon which it appeared.

'One Little Victory' (5.47)
'Distant Early Warning' (5.24)
'Red Barchetta' (7.09)
'Clockwork Angels' (7.46)
'The Wreckers' (5.39)

'The Camera Eye' (10.22)
There are some new introductory sound effects – including a phone and a plane – for the last Rush studio song to break the ten-minute mark, which gets a much heavier interpretation here. The guitar dominates the soundstage. Overall, the song is faster, fierier and sounds more engaging throughout. At the end, with Lee's 'in the city ... yeah ... baby', we have a fresh comedy moment: 'On three – Why you think I have this outrageous accent you silly King?', a line from the 1974 film *Monty Python And The Holy Grail*.

'Losing It' (6.13)
Featuring Jonathan Dinklage from the *Clockwork Angels* String Ensemble in place of Ben Mink, this is a very appropriate choice for the final track to be heard on this epic retrospective live album. Lee's voice has a curious, baritone quality to it, and this adds a layer of dark regret over the song. Dinklage's solo is an accurate and moving reproduction of Mink's work, and the song itself is an excellent anthem to the passing of time.

Exit The Warriors ...

At the end of the final three-song medley of 'What You're Doing'/'Working Man'/'Garden Road' on the last date of the *R40* tour, Lee shouted to the highly charged crowd, 'Thank you so much, Los Angeles! On behalf of the greatest crew and organisation in the world...' It was at this point that a beaming Peart emerged from behind his kit, walked to the front of the stage, wedging himself between Lee and Lifeson to their immense surprise, and took a bow with his friends. It would be the first and last time this happened. Ever the professional, Lee managed to continue: 'On behalf of our whole organisation, thank you, United States of America, for 40 awesome years. And I do hope we'll meet again sometime. Bye-bye.' Peart quietly announced his retirement from drumming and, therefore, from Rush a few months later.

Sadly, despite hopes that a well-earned rest would help rejuvenate the drummer to want to record and play again, Peart's retirement was permanent. This was a major, but necessary decision, and he spent his time with his new family and continued with his writing projects. In the summer of 2016, he was diagnosed with glioblastoma, a form of brain cancer. A subsequent operation extended his life by over 3 years, with Peart dying on 7 January 2020. He was only 67. In a time when secrets rarely remain private, Peart kept the diagnosis to his closest friends and family. The degree of mourning amongst the band's worldwide fan base was amplified by the shock of its announcement.

In addition to winning many awards in a wide variety of drumming publications over the decades, receiving the Order of Canada in 1996 and being inducted in the Canadian Songwriters Hall of Fame in 2010 and the Rock and Roll Hall of Fame in 2013, Peart was also awarded an Honorary Doctorate in Music from Nipissing University, Ontario, in 2014. After his premature death, he was inducted into the Percussive Arts Society in 2020, the same year as the City Council of St Catherines named the pavilion at Lakeside Park, Port Dalhousie, Ontario, in his honour. Adjacent to the pavilion is a bronze statue of Peart and his kit, mid-solo. 'The measure of a life...'

Peart's death also seemingly meant the end of Rush. The trio had always said that 'anything and everything Rush' had to have the agreement of all of them for the work to continue. Without Peart, there could not, and would not, be a band. At the time, Lee was on record as saying that a re-launch of Rush in a post-Peart world would tarnish the band's legacy. However, minds were to be changed, as we shall see.

Both Lee and Lifeson have maintained a presence in rock circles: Lifeson formed a new band, Envy Of None, along with Andy Curran (bass), Maiah Wynne (vocals) and Alfio Annibalini (keyboards). Fans expecting a gritty rock record were in for a surprise when the self-titled studio album appeared in April 2022. It is a moody, introspective, ambient affair, and about as 'Un-Rush' as the guitarist could get. A second album, *Stygian Waves*, emerged in March 2025, offering up more of the same, but this time with greater contributions from Lifeson.

In 2023, Lee published his autobiography *My 'Effin Life*, which is a fascinating and brutally honest account of the man, his life and achievements. On a worldwide book tour, he would sometimes welcome a 'special guest' to join him. His school friend of many decades would once again walk into the limelight to enormous cheers. Seeing the two men on stage but without any guitars was a surreal experience; Lifeson went as far as to be the surprise host at Portsmouth on the United Kingdom leg of his friend's promotional tour.

R50 (2025)

Released on 21 March 2025, *R50* is either a luxurious, career-spanning retrospective with some 'must-have', never-before-released tracks, or a money-making exercise of a box set destined only for the coffee tables and audiophile hi-fi systems of the wealthy Rush absolutist.

This tenth anniversary commemoration of the *R40* tour 'marks the band's half-century in the music business' (according to the promotional blurb). Well, not really. *R40* and the retirement and subsequent death of Peart underlined the fact that Rush, as Alex and Geddy have frequently explained, is over. Rush stopped when their friend died.

This gripe aside (and the fact that the *R40* tour was actually 41 years after their debut album in 1974), the box set showcases the band's incredible musical history and legacy from their very first single to their last live medley of songs. Such indulgence does not come cheap; *R50*, depending on the format chosen, currently ranges in price from circa £80 up to approximately £300. Big money does indeed 'leave a bruise'. The track listing is:

CD One

1: 'Not Fade Away'
2: 'You Can't Fight It'
3: 'Working Man (Vault Edition)'
4: 'Need Some Love'
5: 'Before And After'
6: 'Bad Boy'
7: 'Garden Road'
8: 'Anthem'
9: 'Fly By Night'
10: 'Bastille Day'
11: '2112: Overture/The Temples Of Syrinx'
12: 'By-Tor & The Snow Dog'
13: 'Something For Nothing'

Tracks one and two make up Rush's first single on Moon Records, preceding their debut album. The single rightly died an early death, but is no doubt included here as the true beginning of an illustrious musical career. Track three features an alternate guitar solo, which has previously only been available as a digital single.

Of greater interest are tracks four and five, which were recorded live at the Laura Secord Secondary School, St Catherines, Canada, in May 1974 with original drummer John Rutsey. Similarly, tracks six and seven were recorded live at the Agora Ballroom, Cleveland, Ohio, in August 1974 and feature Peart. Track eight is another live recording, this time from the Electric Lady Studios in New York in December 1974, also presented here for the first time.

The Rush fan will have the remainder of the songs, and herein lies the problem with the majority of the rest of this collection. We already own it. We possibly bought the records when they first came out (on either vinyl or cassette). Maybe we purchased them again in the age of CD, and then possibly a further time in the era of the remastered, anniversary CD versions with bonus live tracks. Rush never had any spare songs discarded on the studio floor. They recorded what they had written for the album, and that was it. So, there are no hidden gems, and whilst the final minutes of the band on stage in 2015 are an emotive rollercoaster, no doubt, it's a lot to spend without getting much that is genuinely fresh in return.

CD Two

14: 'Closer To The Heart'
15: 'Xanadu'
16: 'Drum Solo'
17: 'The Trees (Vault Edition)'
18: 'La Villa Strangiato'
19: 'In The Mood'
20: 'The Spirit Of Radio'
21: 'Natural Science'
22: 'A Passage To Bangkok'
23: 'Tom Sawyer'
24: 'Limelight'
25: 'Vital Signs'

On this CD, the only item of real interest is track 17, which again features an alternative guitar solo. This has never been officially released beyond its appearance in the instrument-based video game *Rock Band*. Tracks 15, 16, 21, 22, 24 and 25 are all live performances taken from existing live albums.

CD Three

26: 'YYZ'
27: 'Subdivisions'
28: 'Red Sector A'
29: 'Witch Hunt'

30: 'New World Man'
31: 'The Big Money'
32: 'Time Stand Still'
33: 'Distant Early Warning'
34: 'Superconductor'
35: 'Dreamline'
36: 'Stick It Out'
37: 'Test For Echo'
38: 'The Rhythm Method'

Tracks 26, 29, 33 and 38 are live performances taken from existing live albums.

CD Four
39: 'One Little Victory'
40: 'Cygnus X-1'
41: 'The Seeker'
42: 'Between The Wheels'
43: 'The Main Monkey Business'
44: 'Workin' Them Angels'
45: 'Freewill'
46: 'Red Barchetta'
47: 'Headlong Flight'
48: 'Manhattan Project'
49: 'Jacob's Ladder'
50: 'What You're Doing'/'Working Man'/'Garden Road'

Track 39 is the 2013 remixed version of the 2002 original. Tracks 40, 42, 44, 45, 46, 48 and 49 are all previously released live recordings. The three songs that constitute the final track are the most interesting and have not been available before; they are the last songs the band played at the last show of the *R40* tour and, with a neat nod to the past, have been newly mixed by Terry Brown.

So, out of 50 tracks, only 12 are new to the ears. Or put another way, the truly dedicated fan already owns 76% of what's on offer here. Is this good value for money, or remuneration for ancient hemp? What else do you get?

A lot of effort has gone into the presentation and packaging. The 'Super Deluxe Edition' ('SDE') includes four CDs, the contents of which are then duplicated over seven LPs. This is puzzling. Why buy it on vinyl and CD? There is plenty of new artwork by, of course, Hugh Syme, who has also created 29 new illustrations that 'celebrate the vibrant essence of Rush's songs', apparently. Also included is a 104-page hardcover book with plenty of photos of the band in action alongside essays from respected rock journalists David Fricke and Philip Wilding.

Exclusive to the 'SDE' are 20 new illustration lithographs by Syme, each one showcasing one song from each studio album. A second hardcover book, a graphic novel, *The Fullness Of Time*, written and illustrated by a company called Fantoons, which 'visually brings to life a conversation between Geddy and Alex reflecting on the trials, tribulations and successes of recording each studio album, with contributions from many of the producers and engineers who were instrumental in the evolution of Rush's sound over the years', completes the package. All of the contents in *R50* are 'housed in a premium box with a rotating lid and a 'Rush 50' golden jubilee emblem.' Great.

The Rush Store Exclusive version of the 'SDE' adds four bonus lithos showing Rush through time, newly illustrated by Fantoons from the characters created for the graphic novel depicting the band across the decades. The third configuration of *R50* is the seven-LP Deluxe Edition with slightly different outer gold graphics, with the hardcover book. The fourth version of *R50* is the four-CD Deluxe Edition, which includes all 50 songs, Syme's artwork and the book. The final configuration is the digital equivalent of the 'SDE'.

On balance, whilst the compilation spans the band's entire recording career from their first-ever single to their final-ever performance, and does include at least one track from each of their studio albums, there isn't enough of genuine interest to make this fan reach for his credit card.

If you want to hear 'Not Fade Away' and 'You Can't Fight It', go to YouTube. A couple of alternate guitar solos in two classic songs? Interesting, but not essential. The rare live performances from the end of Rutsey/beginning of Peart eras are intriguing, but there aren't enough of them. The band had another of their own compositions, 'Fancy Dancer', in their set list during this period, but this seems to have been lost in the mists of time. And 'Bad Boy' isn't a long-lost original song; it was a cover of Larry Williams' 1958 composition.

Now, if all the previously unreleased tracks were put onto a single CD, that would be worth purchasing. But, as it stands, *R50* is a lot to pay for a few things we haven't heard before, a nice big book and some pictures. Not for me, then, but no doubt it will sell by the shed-load. To my mind, it's the first release, with the possible exception of 2009's *Working Men*, to somewhat tarnish the band's legacy.

My personal *R50*, taking two tracks from each studio album and using the live albums as opportunities to include more essential songs in the collection, would be:

CD One – The 1970s

1: 'Finding My Way' (*Rush*)
2: 'Working Man' (*Rush*)
3: 'Anthem' (*Fly By Night*)
4: 'By-Tor And The Snow Dog' (*Fly By Night*)

5: 'Lakeside Park' (*Caress Of Steel*)
6: 'Bacchus Plateau' (*Caress Of Steel*)
7: 'Overture' (*2112*)
8: 'The Temples Of Syrinx' (*2112*)
9: 'Bastille Day' (*All The World's A Stage*)
9: 'A Farewell To Kings' (*A Farewell To Kings*)
10: 'Xanadu' (*A Farewell To Kings*)
12: 'Hemispheres – Prelude' (*Hemispheres*)
13: 'La Villa Strangiato' (*Hemispheres*)

CD Two – The 1980s
14: 'The Spirit Of Radio' (*Permanent Waves*)
15: 'Freewill' (*Permanent Waves*)
16: 'Tom Sawyer' (*Moving Pictures*)
17: 'Red Barchetta' (*Moving Pictures*)
18: 'The Analog Kid' (*Signals*)
19: 'New World Man' (*Signals*)
20: 'Distant Early Warning' (*Grace Under Pressure*)
21: 'Kid Gloves' (*Grace Under Pressure*)
22: 'The Big Money' (*Power Windows*)
23: 'Manhattan Project' (*Power Windows*)
24: 'Hold Your Fire' (*Hold Your Fire*)
25: 'Time Stands Still' (*Hold Your Fire*)
26: 'The Pass' (*Presto*)
27: 'Available Light' (*Presto*)

CD Three – The 1990s
28: 'Dreamline' (*Roll The Bones*)
29: 'Face Up' (*Roll The Bones*)
30: 'Stick It Out' (*Counterparts*)
31: 'Nobody's Hero' (*Counterparts*)
32: 'Test For Echo' (*Test For Echo*)
33: 'Resist' (*Test For Echo*)
34: 'Limelight' (*Different Stages – Live*)
35: 'Driven' (*Different Stages – Live*)
36: 'The Trees' (*Different Stages – Live*)
37: 'Closer To The Heart' (*Different Stages – Live*)
38: 'YYZ' (*Different Stages – Live*)

CD4 – The 2000s And Beyond
39: 'Ceiling Unlimited' (*Vapor Trails*)
40: 'Secret Touch' (*Vapor Trails*)
41: 'Summertime Blues' (*Feedback*)
42: 'Crossroads' (*Feedback*)

43: 'Far Cry' (*Snakes And Arrows*)
44: 'Spindrift' (*Snakes And Arrows*)
45: 'Clockwork Angels' (*Clockwork Angels*)
46: 'The Garden' (*Clockwork Angels*)
47: 'Subdivisions' (*Clockwork Angels Tour*)
48: 'The Anarchist' (*R40 – Live*)
49: 'Headlong Flight' (*R40 – Live*)
50: 'What You're Doing'/'Working Man'/'Garden Road' (*R50*)

As far as I know, only one other person agrees completely with my selection, and that is my proofreader and equally long-time Rush fan Mike Rawsthorne, the Geddy to my Alex, if you will. And even then, we disagree on two of my choices. Everyone else will have a different selection of favourites, and 'Hurrah' to that! There is much to admire in the band's substantial output, and even where I have been critical of individual songs and albums in this book, I have maintained my admiration for the authenticity of their work. Integrity always wins in the long run.

Watching the various live DVD performances Rush issued over their career, it is clear that the band rigorously maintained the same ethos throughout: to deliver the best rock show possible. The productions are as impressive as the music; the songs of the 'reunited' era are packed with as much integrity, intelligence and technique as their earlier songs and the sense of sheer enjoyment in their music is shared by musicians and fans alike. The band were always moving forward, searching for what Geddy once described as the 'best' Rush. In an interview with *Prog* magazine in April 2025, Alex confirmed this, saying: 'Progress is important to us. We always need to go somewhere. We always wanted to evolve.'

In the end, Rush were just three men who made the music they wanted to make in the way they wanted to make it. No histrionics, no blazing rows in the glare of the media, no break-ups and subsequent cash-in reunions, no false 'final tours', no sense that they were just in it for the money. Constantly changing throughout their long career, the band reflected the prevailing musical trends whilst writing and performing compelling, thought-provoking and powerful music to legions of fans across the globe.

Truly, all the world was indeed a stage. But they were not 'merely players, performers, or portrayers'. Alex, Geddy and Neil inspired their fans, both musician and non-musician alike, with their instrumental mastery, songwriting craft, lyrical depth, and positive attitude to become better people. Now, that's a legacy.

Postscript

The 'Fifty Something' Tour: The End Continues?

Peart's death has not, after all, seen the end of Rush; it has meant a hiatus of over a decade. In early October 2025, the band's promotional machine sprang into action with Lee and Lifeson announcing a 2026 tour, *Fifty Something*. This is designed to be a 'celebration of Rush's music, legacy and the life of late drummer and lyricist Neil Peart.' Commenting on the two-thirds reunion, Geddy said:

> It's been over ten years since Alex and I have performed the music of Rush alongside our fallen bandmate and friend, Neil. A lifetime's worth of songs that we had put our cumulative hearts and souls into writing, recording and playing together onstage. And so, after all that has gone down since that last show, Alex and I have done some serious soul searching and come to the decision that we fucking miss it, and that it's time for a celebration of 50-something years of Rush music. So, in 2026, my BFF Lerxst (aka Alex Lifeson) and I are going to hit the road once again to pay tribute to our past and to Neil by performing a vast selection of Rush songs in a handful of cities. No small task, because as we all know, Neil was irreplaceable.

The vacant drum is to be filled by a female drummer from Germany, who has performed with Jeff Beck and released four solo albums. She was born on 29 May 1983, between the release of *Signals* and *Grace Under Pressure*. This may make some readers feel very old! She's only 43!

Geddy continued:

> Yet, life is full of surprises, and we have been introduced to another remarkable person, an incredible drummer and musician who is adding another chapter to our story while continuing her own fascinating musical journey. Her name is Anika Nilles, and we could not be more excited to introduce her to our loyal and dedicated Rush fanbase, who, we know, will give her every chance to live up to that near-impossible role. Before we hit the stage, we also hope to add another musician or two to expand our sound a wee bit and free up Alex and me, in order to show off some of our new fancy dance steps.
>
> Lerxst, Anika and I, along with many of our longstanding crew members, have been hard at work rehearsing and designing the kind of Rush show you've grown accustomed to expect from us. We dearly hope you will come along and help us celebrate our history together.

Lee and Lifeson have naturally approached the drummer's widow and daughter, Carrie Nuttall-Peart and Olivia Peart, regarding the tour, and they have given their whole-hearted backing, saying:

> We are thrilled to support the *Fifty Something* tour, celebrating a band whose music has resonated and inspired fans for generations, and to honour Neil's extraordinary legacy as both a drummer and lyricist. Neil's musicianship was singular. Compositions of intricacy and power that expanded what rhythm itself could express. As both drummer and lyricist, he was irreplaceable. Inimitable in his artistry and unmatched in the depth and imagination he brought to the lyrics that inspired and moved so many, he profoundly shaped how fans connected with him and the band, giving voice and meaning to their own lives. As the band enter this new chapter, it promises to be truly unforgettable. We are excited to see how their new vision unfolds, and to hear this legendary music played live once again.

Almost as soon as the tour was announced, additional dates were added. And then even more. Currently, the *Fifty Something* tour consists of 58 concerts in cities across Canada, the United States and Mexico, commencing on 7 June and finishing on 17 December 2026. Almost certainly, another live album/DVD package will be released for those of us unlucky enough not to get tickets to enjoy the reunited experience as well.

Could this revitalised Rush release any brand new music? Peart, the copious writer, left many sets of lyrics behind, words which, at the time, were initially put to one side by Lee and Lifeson, but could have been stored away as future possibilities. Peart had said that over the decades, plenty of possibilities were sent to the pair, but relatively few were accepted. Could there be a new Rush album with old Peart lyrics? Time, never one to stand still, will tell.

In the end, the *Fifty Something* tour is about two men, best friends since school days, who have shared a love of music *and* been in the 'world's biggest cult band' for decades, getting together and playing the music they love together once more. And that is something to be celebrated: friendship, creativity and a lifelong love of music. Geddy and Alex (and Anika, of course) ... go for it!

Would you like to write for Sonicbond Publishing?

We are mainly a music publisher, but we also occasionally publish in other genres including film and television. At Sonicbond Publishing we are always on the look-out for authors, particularly for our two main series, On Track and Decades.

Mixing fact with in depth analysis, the On Track series examines the entire recorded work of a particular musical artist or group. All genres are considered from easy listening and jazz to 60s soul to 90s pop, via rock and metal.

The Decades series singles out a particular decade in an artist or group's history and focuses on that decade in more detail than may be allowed in the On Track series.

While professional writing experience would, of course, be an advantage, the most important qualification is to have real enthusiasm and knowledge of your subject. First-time authors are welcomed, but the ability to write well in English is essential.

Sonicbond Publishing has distribution throughout Europe and North America, and all our books are also published in E-book form. Authors will be paid a royalty based on sales of their book. Further details about our books are available from www.sonicbondpublishing.com. To contact us, complete the contact form there or email info@sonicbondpublishing.co.uk